W.D Andrews

Swimming and Life-Saving

W.D Andrews

Swimming and Life-Saving

ISBN/EAN: 9783337311735

Printed in Europe, USA, Canada, Australia, Japan

Cover: Foto ©Lupo / pixelio.de

More available books at **www.hansebooks.com**

SWIMMING AND LIFE-SAVING

BY

CAPT. W. D. ANDREWS, G.C.V.,

Of the Dominion of Canada Life-Saving Service; Gold Life-Saving Medallist of the First Class;
Medallist of the Royal Humane Society, etc., etc.

TRUE HEROISM.

"We honor our soldiers, 'but what of the men
   Whose deeds of cool daring in fire and in flood
Have saved precious lives, yes, again and again?
For these can we say, we have done what we could?
The brave fellows, thrilled with humanity's cry,
   Have plunged in the water, or rushed through the flame,
And quick to the rescue to save life or die,
   Are heroes, who never need blush at the name.'"

                      —ROBERT AWDE.

TORONTO:
WILLIAM BRIGGS, 78 & 80 KING STREET EAST.
C. W. COATES, Montreal, Que.   S. F. HUESTIS, Halifax, N.S.
1889.

> " Whether from Scotland's hills of broom,
>   Or France's vine-clad capes serene ;
> Whether from England's fields of bloom,
>   Or Ireland's vales of emerald green ;
> Assembled on St. Lawrence brink,
>   We stand together, man to man,
> And all our vain distinctions sink
>   In the proud name, 'CANADIAN.' "
>
> —*Canadian Gazette.*

TO THE

PEOPLE OF CANADA

THIS BOOK IS

Respectfully Dedicated

WITH THE BEST WISHES OF

THE AUTHOR.

PREFACE.

"He that saveth a human life is greater than one who taketh a city."
—*Confucius.*

SWIMMING may be considered both as an enjoyable pastime and an invigorating bodily exercise; but as a means of preserving life, it has the greatest claim upon the attention of the public. Upon our ability to swim, sometimes, depends our chances of saving our own life and, possibly, the lives of others. It is one of the most essential features in physical education, and it should never be left to the choice of our youth to acquire the art; its practice should be inculcated as an absolute duty. A knowledge of swimming, both theoretical and practical, should be included in the education of every person, irrespective of age or sex. In the schools of France and Germany every scholar receives instruction in the art of swimming.

During the many years I have been connected with the Life-Saving Service I have met with hundreds of persons who were unable to swim, and now that loss of sight compels me to rest on my oars for a time, at least, I embrace the opportunity of putting into book-form the numerous notes I have made from time to time on this subject, with the hope that it may be the means of instructing many in this useful accomplishment.

W. D. A.

ACKNOWLEDGMENTS.

"A friend in need, is a friend indeed."—*Old Proverb.*

OWING to my loss of sight, it was necessary for me, in arranging for the printer the manuscript I had previously written, to avail myself of the help of a companion in the General Hospital, who could see to make such alterations as I might suggest. A feeling of gratitude, therefore, prompts me to acknowledge the services rendered me in this respect by Mr. HOWELL, who kindly acted as my amanuensis, faithfully transcribing every word as it fell from my lips, and assisting materially in the arrangement of the matter. Believing that object-lessons will assist the reader, I have myself posed in all the various positions in swimming, floating, plunging, etc., with a view to explaining my ideas more clearly.

I embrace this opportunity of expressing my sincere thanks to the friends who stood by me during my affliction, to whom I have much pleasure in addressing the following lines:

> Who in my hour of greatest need, when others passed me by,
> Did prove themselves my friends, indeed, in trouble ever nigh.
> 'Tis when the heart is desolate, its inmost thoughts unfold,
> And we can justly separate the dross from the pure gold.
> When the sun of prosperity upon my pathway shone,
> They gathered 'round me merrily, brimful of mirth and fun;
> But when the hour of trial came, they very soon withdrew,
> Except a few, worthy the name, who stood by firm and true.
> Should Providence restore my sight, and I my health regain,
> I'll strive to weld the links aright in friendship's golden chain.
>
> —W. D. A.

GENERAL HOSPITAL, TORONTO,
  Christmas, 1888.

CONTENTS.

CHAPTER	PAGE
I.—THE ART OF SWIMMING	11
II.—A CHAT WITH THE LADIES	12
A Brave Young Lady	14
III.—A WORD FOR THE BOYS	15
"I Can Swim, Sir"	16
IV.—PHYSICAL TRAINING	16
V.—PHYSICAL DEVELOPMENT	18
VI.—A YARN FOR SEAMEN	19
VII.—OUR LIGHTHOUSES	20
VIII.—SELECTING A SUITABLE BATHING PLACE	21
IX.—THE DANGER OF WEEDS	22
How to Extricate One's Self from Weeds	23
X.—BATHING	23
Rules of the Royal Humane Society	25
XI.—A TALK WITH THE PUBLIC SCHOOL BOARD	25
XII.—ARTIFICIAL AIDS TO SWIMMING	27
XIII.—THE BUOYANCY OF WATER	28
XIV.—THE NECESSITY OF CONFIDENCE	28
XV.—HOW TO ACQUIRE CONFIDENCE	29
XVI.—THE DANGER OF CRAMPS	30
The Remedy for Cramps	30
XVII.—DEFORMITY NO IMPEDIMENT TO ACQUIRING THE ART OF SWIMMING	31
XVIII.—BREAST STROKE	32
XIX.—BREAST SWIMMING	35
XX.—SWIMMING ON THE BACK	35
XXI.—SIDE STROKE	39
XXII.—"HAND OVER HAND"	42
XXIII.—THE DOG STROKE	43
XXIV.—THE INDIAN STROKE	44
XXV.—FLOATING	45
Horizontal Floating	46
Perpendicular Floating	46
XXVI.—TREADING WATER	46

CONTENTS.

CHAPTER	PAGE
XXVII.—Jumping into the Water	49
XXVIII.—Plunging	49
The Low Plunge	51
The Popular Plunge	52
The High Plunge	52
XXIX.—The "Header"	54
The Running Header	55
The Skimming Plunge	55
XXX.—Swimming Under Water	56
XXXI.—Diving	57
XXXII.—Swimming in Clothes	60
XXXIII.—Upright Swimming	61
XXXIV.—French Swimming Drill	62
XXXV.—German Swimming Schools	63
An Anecdote of "Our Fritz"	65
XXXVI.—Ornamental Swimming	66
To Swim Without Using Either Hand	67
On the Back, Feet First, Without Using the Feet	68
On the Back, Head First, Without Using the Feet	68
Backwards on the Breast	68
Semi-Somersaults	69
Somersaults	69
Leap-Frog	70
The Steamer	71
The Propeller	71
The Pendulum	72
The Spinning Top	72
The Washing-Tub	72
Wrestling in the Water	73
Boxing in the Water	74
The Revolving Feat	75
To Swim Holding One Foot	75
Holding the Feet in One or Both Hands	76
Hurdle Races	76
Egg Hunt	76
Duck Hunt	77
Tub Race	77
Water Polo	77
XXXVII.—Learning to Swim with the Aid of a Teacher	78
XXXVIII.—Public Swimming Schools	80
Encouragement of Swimming at Public Schools	81
XXXIX.—Public Swimming Baths	82
The Wiman Island Swimming Baths	82
The West End Island Baths	83
The Y. M. C. A. Baths, Toronto	85

CONTENTS.

CHAPTER	PAGE
XL.—SWIMMING RACES	85
XLI.—SWIMMING CLUBS	87
The Amateur Swimming Association of Great Britain	87
The Liverpool Swimming Club	87
The Ilex Swimming Club	87
The Montreal Swimming Club	88
The Dolphin Swimming Club, Toronto	88
Officers of the Dolphin Swimming Club	89
Rules of the Dolphin Swimming Club	91
XLII.—THE PROPER METHOD TO BE ADOPTED IN RESCUING DROWNING PERSONS BY SWIMMING TO THEIR RELIEF	92
XLIII.—DIRECTIONS FOR RESTORING THE APPARENTLY DROWNED, RECOMMENDED BY THE DOLPHIN SWIMMING CLUB	96
XLIV.—THE ROYAL HUMANE SOCIETY	100
Description of the Medals and Clasps of the Royal Humane Society	104
XLV.—THE MASSACHUSETTS HUMANE SOCIETY	105
XLVI.—ROYAL NATIONAL LIFE-BOAT INSTITUTION	107
XLVII.—THE LIFE-SAVING BENEVOLENT ASSOCIATION OF NEW YORK	108
XLVIII.—THE ALBERT MEDAL	109
XLIX.—UNITED STATES LIFE-SAVING SERVICE	112
L.—OUR LIFE-SAVING SERVICE	113
The Life-Boat	114
LI.—LIFE-SAVING APPLIANCES	114
LII.—THE LYLE GUN	117
McLellan's Apparatus Waggon	117
LIII.—THE DOBBINS LIFE-BOAT	119
LIV.—ALWAYS READY	124
The Operation of Rescue	126
The Square and Compass	128
LV.—"ONE OF THE MEN WE KNOW"	129

ILLUSTRATIONS.

	PAGE
Frontispiece	
Ladies in Bathing Costumes	13
Ladies Diving	58
Learning to Swim with the Aid of a Teacher	79
Association Hall, Toronto	84
Medals and Clasps of the Royal Humane Society	103
The Lyle Gun and McLellan's Apparatus Waggon	116
Launch of the Dobbins Life-Boat	118
Landing in the Surf	121
Going to the Rescue	123

With seventy-eight minor illustrations.

SWIMMING AND LIFE-SAVING.

CHAPTER I.

THE ART OF SWIMMING.

> "This is the purest exercise of health,
> The kind refresher of the summer heats."
> —*Thomson's* "*Seasons.*"

THE primary object of this work is the extension of a knowledge of swimming, with a view to the preservation of life from drowning.

Many persons never think of the value of swimming, until by some unforeseen accident they are precipitated into the water; then instantly and unpleasantly they are effectually convinced of the importance of the art.

To know how to swim is very necessary in a country like Canada, where there is so much boating, and where so many young persons, inexperienced in the handling of boats, are to be found at any time during the summer season upon the water.

Water employments, water amusements, and water accidents, all tell in the same direction; all point to the urgent necessity there exists for a more extended knowledge of the art of swimming.

As swimming is an art, it has laws and rules the same as any other gymnastic exercise, which, if properly understood, will enable the novice to sustain his body, and to navigate in the water at pleasure.

The author proposes to advert to those rules, and so to simplify them by words and illustrations as to render the learner all the book assistance possible, which, if faithfully followed, will eventually lead to his becoming a good and successful swimmer.

Some people have an idea that in order to effect a rescue a person should be very strong, and above the ordinary size. The real truth of the matter is, large men stand like pillars and move like oxen. Some of the men whom, under Providence, I have been enabled to rescue from drowning, were much larger and heavier than myself. Skill and dexterity are the primary essentials in life-saving.

CHAPTER II.

A CHAT WITH THE LADIES.

" Go where the fair water-nymphs bathe,
   In grottoes by the sea,
 Where mermaids sport upon the wave,
   And gambol joyously."

Ladies number largely among the excursionists that crowd the many pleasure steamers which throng our harbors, and patronize the numerous flotillas of small boats that are to be found at every lake and seaside resort in Canada, and surely the saving of their lives is a matter worth taking into consideration. The writer has, therefore, deemed it advisable to address this chapter to ladies especially, with the hope that they will derive benefit from the perusal of it.

Women and girls are usually so terrified when they find themselves precipitated into the water that they lose all self-control, and cling

Ladies in Bathing Costumes.

frantically to some person who is trying to save them, thus greatly endangering the would-be rescuer's life, even though he be an expert swimmer.

I can speak from experience in this matter, for among the many persons whom it has been my privilege to rescue at various times, were a number of ladies, who invariably clung to me in such a manner as greatly to impede my progress and endanger both their lives and my own.

Regarding the best style of bathing-suit for ladies, the accompanying full-page illustration gives front and back view of the most popular bathing costume. It is generally known as the combination suit, *i.e.*, the drawers and waist are in one piece. The skirt being an extra garment, to be worn to and from the water, and removed while in the water. My lady pupils usually followed this method, as it gave them the greatest freedom in their swimming exercises. This neat bathing dress can be braided or otherwise ornamented, according to the taste of the fair wearer.

. Many of my young lady pupils found it advantageous to dispense with the short sleeves altogether, leaving the armholes simply like a gentleman's vest, with colored binding added, according to taste. This is certainly a decided improvement, as it gives much greater freedom to the arms and shoulders while swimming. Shoes ought always to be at hand in the event of the shore being rough or pebbly, and to avoid all accidents.

A Brave Young Lady.

As an incentive to ladies to enter more heartily into the exercise of swimming, I have much pleasure in recording here a gallant rescue effected by Miss Mabel Andrews, on 22nd June, 1887. Two children were in imminent danger of drowning in the Beaver River, near Meaford, Grey County, Ontario, when Miss Andrews, seeing their danger, plunged in with her clothes on, and succeeded in bringing the children safe to shore. This act, by a lady only sixteen years old, was truly noble, and the Royal Humane Society awarded her their bronze medal, which was most appropriately presented by our esteemed Mayor, E. F. Clarke, M.P.P.

CHAPTER III.

A WORD FOR THE BOYS.

> "The school-boys of the water feel,
> And where the stream is warmest,
> Upon the bank they quickly peel,
> And plunge right in head foremost ;
> O'er bathing suits they make no fuss,
> Their texture or their trimming,
> In purest *naturalibus*
> That's how they go in swimming."

Until the public swimming baths become more numerous, boys should be permitted to bathe in our lakes and rivers without molestation.

Half the papers you pick up nowadays have appeals to authorities of one sort and another to protect society from the small boy, who persists in going in swimming without clothes on. Society, of course, ought to be protected, but, on the other hand, the boys ought to swim. It is their nature to do so. It is odd that it never occurs to society to "look the other way" when the boys are about to swim. That would perfectly protect society, the boys, the authorities and the newspapers. It seems like an easy thing to do ; but, in practice, society, or a part of it, finds it very hard to do, in fact, quite impossible. And society has been like that for one hundred years. It was a little longer ago than that that a solid Pennsylvania Dutchman came into the presence of the commander of the British troops, then occupying Philadelphia, and complained that the soldiers had a habit of going to swim within sight of his house, to the great annoyance of his daughters. The General promised to look into it. The officer sent to examine reported that the swimming place was so far from the house that the men could not be seen. So they were allowed to continue. The Dutch father came again to complain, and when told of the officer's report, replied, "Ah, but those girls have got a spy-glass." Let the boys get health and fun in the water, and let society focus its spy-glass in some other direction.

Aelia tells a charming story of the boys, who in their bathing made the friendship of a "Dolphin," and used to ride shoreward on his broad back.

"I Can Swim, Sir."

The following naval story is recorded for the benefit of the boys. During the celebrated naval engagement between the Dutch and English, the British Admiral, finding himself assailed by two of the enemy, thought it prudent to call for assistance, which was near, although communication by signal was impossible, owing to the density of the smoke from the heavy cannonading. In his extremity he called for volunteers to convey a despatch by swimming, and among the number who immediately responded was his own cabin boy. The Admiral, addressing the brave lad, asked him, "What can you do?" The boy answered, touching his cap, "I can swim, sir." This answer induced the Admiral to trust the lad to carry out the dangerous duty, which he did successfully, notwithstanding the continuous showers of shot and shell. The object was attained by the Captain, to whom the boy delivered his orders, bearing down to his admiral's relief; and so the Dutch were defeated. The Admiral, addressing the boy in the presence of the officers and crew, said with much earnestness, taking him by the hand, and thanking him for his bravery, "I shall live to see you an admiral some day." The prophecy was fulfilled. The boy became Admiral Cloudesley Shovel, and was knighted by the King.

I have very great pleasure in here adding a highly meritorious act of bravery performed by a Toronto lad of my acquaintance, he being only ten years old. Leonard T. Jillard, on the 2nd July, 1888, at the eastern point of the Island, seeing one of his companions sink and in great danger, jumped in, and diving succeeded in catching the boy and landing him safely on shore. A number of bystanders who witnessed his bravery presented him with small sums. This boy had taken lessons from the author.

CHAPTER IV.

PHYSICAL TRAINING.

"The boy is father of the man."
—*Old Proverb.*

Believing in the truth of the above quotation, I address this chapter more particularly to the rising generation, but older heads may read it with profit. Hitherto I have tried to avoid, as far as I could, consistently with the nature of this work, the too frequent use of the personal pronoun, not wishing to appear egotistical. In this chapter, however, I will adopt the conversational style, as it will be much easier thereby to convey my ideas on this important subject. Knowing that the mind is intimately associated with the body, my first advice to all who wish to become athletes is to avoid the use of intoxicating liquors, which have a tendency to weaken the intellect and enfeeble the body. There are plenty of wholesome beverages which will supply all you want in this respect, and at the same time leave the head clear and the body strong. Next, avoid the use of tobacco, not only on account of its uncleanliness, but also because the nicotine it contains is liable to poison the blood. Providence never intended that man should chew like a cow or smoke like a chimney. Again, avoid reading trashy literature, which has a pernicious effect on so many of our youth. There are plenty of journals that cater for the wants of young people, such as the "Boys' Own Paper," and similar periodicals, which have a healthy and elevating influence. Above all, boys, avoid becoming a "dude." To sensible men and women there is nothing more contemptible than these effeminate creatures, with their "snobbish" dress, hair parted in the centre, cane and eye-glass, and other external signs of lack of brains within. So long as Providence gives you health and strength and the use of your limbs, no cane is required, and while you enjoy the blessing of sight you need not use an eye-glass. Endeavor to cultivate a spirit of self-reliance, be honest and truthful in dealing with your comrades. Don't "peach" on your associates, but endeavor to observe the golden rule of "Doing unto others as you would they should do unto you." So much for the training of the mind. Now for the bodily training. Sleep on a hard bed, bathe regularly, eat plain, wholesome food, with plenty of fruit for dessert, avoid pastry and sweetmeats of all kinds, take plenty of open-air exercise daily when weather permits—walking up-hill will expand the lungs wonderfully. These directions, if faithfully observed, will enable you to become a healthy and vigorous man. Remember that the God-given Cordon of Brain is more valuable than the Ribbons of the Bath or Garter.

CHAPTER V.

PHYSICAL DEVELOPMENT.

"Quit you like men, be strong."—*St. Paul.*

Boys—Above all things endeavor to be "manly." Canadians are rapidly taking their place in all athletic competitions. Our oarsmen, swimmers, runners, fencers, and athletes generally, will compare favorably with the best the world can produce; while in lacrosse, cricket, baseball, lawn tennis, and other games, we frequently take the lead. In order to become an athlete, it is absolutely necessary that all kinds of intemperance and excesses should be avoided. When possible, the morning bath in cold water, immediately on rising, should begin the day's exercises; a handful or two of salt thrown into the water will prevent your taking cold; rub vigorously with a coarse Turkish towel, until the body and limbs are in a healthy glow. If time permits, a short walk before breakfast will restore the circulation and produce a keen appetite for the morning meal.

For the development of the chest, the horizontal bar is very valuable. Constant practice will enable you to increase the number of times you can breast the bar consecutively without touching the ground, when suspended at arms' length. The author, after four years' practice, was able to do this twenty-seven times without resting. Nature permits no vacuum, and as this exercise tends to expand the chest, the lungs are proportionately inflated. Some of my pupils have been able to increase their chest measurement fully four inches by this method of training.

Rowing machines, dumb-bells, Indian clubs, parallel bars, and other gymnastic appliances, when used regularly, all contribute to the development of the human frame. These, however, must be used systematically, and not spasmodically, in order to obtain any actual benefit. The following anecdote may here prove interesting. Shortly after the Declaration of Independence by the American Colonists, the officials of a New England college asked permission from a celebrated Indian chief to train six boys belonging to his tribe. This permission was readily granted, the boys remaining under their white tutors five or six years. Shortly after their return to their own tribe, the Indian chief appeared at the white settlement. "Friends," said he, "we are grateful for your intended kindness, but when our boys came back to us they were poor runners, unable to endure fatigue; poor hunters, unskilled in the use of the bow and arrow; and were entirely unfit for life in the woods. To show our appreciation of your kindness, however, I would ask you, in the name of my tribe, to let us have a number of your boys, for several years, *that we may make men of them.*" While I would not underrate the value of education, still we must remember that "All work and no play makes Jack a dull boy." Wellington used to say that the school play-ground was the nucleus from which Great Britain drew her heroes. The same may be said of every nation.

CHAPTER VI.

A YARN FOR SEAMEN.

" Never, I ween, did swimmer,
　　In such an evil case,
　Struggle through such a raging flood,
　　Safe to the landing place;
　But his limbs were borne up bravely,
　　By the brave heart within,
　And our good father Tiber,
　　Bore bravely up his chin."
　　　　—*Macaulay's Lays of Ancient Rome.*

To those who have ever been at sea for any length of time, it is almost entirely unnecessary to advance anything to show the immense advantage of a knowledge of the art of swimming.

So fully has this fact been recognized by the maritime powers, that one of the first qualifications for employment in the Marine Service is a knowledge of swimming.

The curriculum of all training ships includes instruction in this valuable accomplishment. The wisdom of this arrangement is fully demonstrated by the following incident:

When H. M. training ship *Goliath* took fire a few years ago, and was burned to the water's edge, not a soul was lost, although there were on board at the time between four and five hundred boys; all swam safely to shore. The loss of life, under these trying circumstances, must have been great were it not for the training the boys had received in the art of swimming · further comment is unnecessary.

The many and frequent disasters on our lakes, rivers, and sea coasts fully demonstrate the necessity there exists for our sailors being taught to swim. Beyond all doubt a great many of the valuable lives sacrificed in past years by these calamities might have been saved had the crews of the ill-fated vessels been taught swimming, even in a moderate degree. These remarks apply not only to the navigating portion of the crews of vessels, steamers, etc., but also to engineers, firemen, stewards and others, composing the ship's company. The great number of officers and seamen who possess the medals of the Royal Humane Society and other decorations for bravery in saving life from drowning, fully demonstrate the immense value of the art to those who follow the sea as a profession. There can hardly be any decoration that a man could receive more honorable than those conferred for saving life.

Among the naval officers who have won deserved honor for bravery in saving life, the name of Captain Lord Charles Beresford, R.N., stands pre-eminent. On two occasions he gallantly plunged overboard and rescued two seamen, for which he received the bronze medal and clasp of the Royal Humane Society, and the silver medal of the Royal National Life-Boat Institution.

Ensign Lovell K. Reynolds, U.S.N., has also distinguished himself in the saving of life from drowning. While on board the U. S. frigate *Constellation* he rescued a crew of twelve men belonging to the Austrian barque *Olira* under circumstances of considerable danger, for which he received a gold life-saving medal of the first class, the Massachusetts Humane Society's gold medal, gold medal from the Benevolent Life-Saving Association of New York, and an Austrian Imperial decoration.

CHAPTER VII.

OUR LIGHTHOUSES.

"Let your lower lights be burning;
Send a gleam across the wave;
Some poor, helpless, struggling seaman,
You may rescue, you may save."
—*Sankey's Hymns.*

The lighthouse system of Canada is superior to any other in the world, for this reason, that it is free, not only to our own people, but to all other nationalities.

All other nations levy a fee on all vessels entering their ports. The lighthouse men of Canada should be supplied with sufficient life-saving apparatus, in case of accident in their vicinity.

The Lighthouse.

Upon a stormy rock-bound coast,
  A lonely lighthouse stands;
Its snow-white walls—the keeper's boast,
  The work of his own hands.

Its strong reflectors brightly shine
  Out o'er the ocean wide;
Here all his energies combine,—
  The lamp's his special pride.

Out o'er the deep, it shines afar,
  With steady light, and true,
The roving seaman's guiding star,
  The safeguard of the crew.

What though tempestuous waves assail
  This sentinel of the sea,
Secure amidst the storm and gale,
  It shines on cheerily.

So may my lamp burn brightly still,
  Supplied with Oil Divine,
And, like the lighthouse on the hill,
  Out in the darkness shine.
                    —W. D. A.

CHAPTER VIII.

SELECTING A SUITABLE BATHING PLACE.

Great care should be exercised in the selection of a bathing place. The novice should choose some well-known bathing resort, where the water is shallow; and, if a stranger, he should sound the chosen spot carefully with a pole, in order to ascertain its depth, since the eye is not always to be relied on in judging the actual depth of water. The kind of place best suited for bathing is on a shelving, sandy shore, on which water gradually deepens, and where no awkward sweep of the current may take the bather off his feet; a smooth, sandy bottom, is to be preferred above all others, as it is much safer and more pleasant in every respect.

The nature of the bottom is of great importance to the novice, and, indeed, to every bather, for the river bed is often composed of sharp stones that cut the feet, or strewn with sunken branches, that thrust their jagged points as if on purpose to wound the unwary bather, and give him a chance of severe injury. Few accidents are more dangerous than those caused by sharp splinters entering the feet, and remaining there. Other waters, and especially those of ponds, and all still waters, deposit a depth of mud at the bottom, which frequently contains substances that treacherously pierce the feet, or perchance cut them dangerously. The mud itself, if shallow, is perfectly harmless, but it is sometimes deep enough to be dangerous. There is yet one other important danger to be guarded against. The bather should be certain that the river-bed contains no deep holes, or other sudden depressions, before he ventures into an unknown stream, as many novices, while attempting to learn how to swim in a place with which they were unacquainted, have lost their lives through accidentally stepping into an unseen hole in the bed of the river. The bather, therefore, should select a bathing place free from holes, weeds, stones, and a muddy bottom, in order to ensure safety. By choosing a place where the water is clear, and deepens gradually, such as a shelving, sandy beach, on a calm day, the novice can banish all fear of drowning from his mind. Should the banks of the bathing place be shaded by a few trees, and should there be, close by, an open space for a run on the grass after the bath, so much the better; and the young learner will then have every inducement to venture the "sudden dip" or "headlong plunge."

CHAPTER IX.

THE DANGER OF WEEDS.

"Seekest thou the plashy brink of reedy lake,
   Or marge of river wide?"
                              —*Bryant.*

Weeds are a great annoyance to bathers, and should be avoided as much as possible, especially by novices. The water-lily must, perforce, rank among weeds in this particular instance, being so considered by swimmers, for it is a very dangerous plant to bathers, on account of its long flower-like stalks which entwine themselves around the bathers' limbs like lassoes, and the leaf-stalks, which are apt to hitch themselves on an arm or leg with unpleasant firmness. The bather, therefore, should select a place which is free from weeds, either attached to the bottom, and scarcely seen from the bank, or floating on the surface.

How to Extricate One's Self from Weeds.

Should the bather, unfortunately, get among weeds, the best way to get clear of their embrace is by "creeping," which method of swimming will be found on page 43, Fig. 20. He must also be very careful not to struggle, as he will thus become more entangled, and may thereby endanger his life; but if he finds himself arrested by a weed, he should lay quietly in the water, keeping himself afloat with one hand, while with the other he unwinds the weed which retards his progress; and on no account become excited, as that would only make matters worse; but he should endeavor to keep as cool as possible, for it is only by preserving presence of mind that the difficulty can be successfully overcome.

To Pass Successfully Over Weeds.

If a bather is in a river where weeds are abundant, and it is desirable to pass over them, he had better swim with the stream, for the weeds, from the force of the current, always point in the direction in which the stream is flowing. By assuming the position described in Horizontal Swimming (see page 35, Fig. 5), the body is raised so near the surface that he will be enabled to pass successfully over the weeds with comparatively little danger or difficulty. It would be advisable also for the swimmer to follow the direction of the stream when diving among weeds, should he ever have occasion to do so; but it will be best to give all weedy and marshy places as wide a berth as possible.

CHAPTER X.

BATHING.

"Go and wash in Jordan seven times, and thy flesh shall come again to thee, and thou shalt be clean."—2 *Kings* v. 10.

It were well for mankind if the prophetic command given to Naaman were followed more generally with reference to our bodily health.

"Cleanliness is next to Godliness," so says the old proverb. This was fully realized under the Mosaic dispensation, as we learn from Holy Writ that the Jews bathed regularly in running waters, and washing was generally interwoven with the Temple ceremonies. The ancients had recourse to their famous rivers for bathing constantly, and it appears many countries required their citizens to comply with the practice, as absolutely necessary, not only to health, but also to the full development of the physical faculties of the human body, and applied to both sexes. The public and private baths of the Romans were particularly luxurious. As far back as the year 312 B.C., the Pricina Publica, or public baths, were constructed near the Circus Maximus, in the Roman capital. These baths had an abundant and constant supply of pure water from the Appian aqueduct. Next, small public, as well as private, baths were constructed, and with the Empire more luxurious forms of bathing were introduced, and warm baths became more popular.

The Canadian people are, as a rule, cleanly in their habits; yet there are many among us who, from the want of proper facilities for indulging in the luxury of a bath, have never been washed since their mothers performed that operation upon them in the old "family tub." A very moderate acquaintance with the nature and action of the skin is sufficient to prove that bathing ought not to be regarded as a luxury, but as an absolute necessity to preserving the organs of the body in a state of health, and it is the best possible preventive for warding off colds with, too often, all their serious consequences.

The immense extension of the city of Toronto within the last few years, with its corresponding increase of manufacturing concerns, has drawn quite an army of mechanics and their assistant workers to reside with us. The nature of their hard work renders a full bath frequently necessary; but until very recently there was no public bath available for them. Now that the Victoria Bath is open to the public, on Huron St., there is little doubt but so great a boon will soon be largely enjoyed, and as the benefits conferred become more thoroughly appreciated, no doubt the erection of other baths will be proceeded with from time to time as necessity is shown to exist in the different districts of the city.

The good example set by the "Queen City of the West" in this most important matter, it is hoped, will be extensively followed by other cities and towns in Canada.

Rules for Bathing as recommended by the Royal Humane Society.

Avoid bathing within two hours after a meal.

Avoid bathing when exhausted by fatigue, or from any other cause.

Avoid bathing when the body is cooling after perspiration.

Avoid bathing altogether in the open air, if, after being a short time in the water, it causes a sense of chilliness, with numbness in the hands and feet.

Bathe when the body is warm, provided no time is lost in getting into the water.

Avoid chilling the body by sitting or standing *undressed* on the banks or in boats after having been in the water.

Avoid remaining too long in the water. Leave the water immediately there is the slightest feeling of chilliness.

The vigorous and strong may bathe early in the morning on an empty stomach.

The young, and those who are weak, had better bathe two or three hours after a meal. The best time for such is from two to three hours after breakfast.

Those who are subject to attacks of giddiness, or faintness, and those who suffer from palpitation and other sense of discomfort at the heart, should not bathe without first consulting their medical adviser.

CHAPTER XI.

A TALK WITH THE PUBLIC SCHOOL BOARD.

"Pro Bono Publico."

Gentlemen,—I have frequently pointed out through the columns of the press the urgent necessity that exists for better facilities for instructing the public school children in the art of swimming. With this object still in view, I address this chapter to you in the hope that you will give it your earnest consideration. I would respectfully suggest that a suitable building be erected in a central portion of the city, easy of access by the street cars, in which a stream of water will be constantly flowing in and out of the plunge-bath. The bath should be of a graduated depth—say three feet at the farthest extremity—deepening to nine feet at the entrance to the building. The water could thus be run off into the street drain by the aid of a sluice-gate. By having life-lines stretched across the bath where the water would be five feet deep, novices could be kept in the shallow part until sufficiently accomplished to enter the deeper water. The city should furnish the water "gratis." The school children should come in classes in regular rotation, according to the seniority of the schools, within specified hours; girls and boys on alternate days. Private and shower baths could be provided for adults, with toilet requisites, on payment of a small fee. During the hours the baths are open the public to be also admissible on payment of the arranged fees. By this plan a knowledge of swimming would become very widely spread. Swimming competitions should be held at frequent intervals, and prizes offered for proficiency in the art; thus inducing perseverance on the part of the pupils to attain the greatest possible efficiency. The following incident will serve to illustrate the necessity of acquiring a knowledge of swimming: A Professor in an English college one day engaged a boatman to row him across a river. On the way he asked the boatman if he learned astronomy. The oarsman confessed his ignorance of that science, whereupon the learned Professor informed him that he had lost one-third of his life in consequence. Again the Professor inquired if he understood mathematics; the answer once more being in the negative. This evoked the assurance of the Professor that another third of the boatman's life was lost. The boatman becoming embarrassed at the enumeration of his losses in the past, neglected his duty, and the boat striking a hidden obstruction was capsized, and both its occupants were struggling in the water. The boatman now became the interrogator, and shouted to the Professor, "Can you swim?" "No, I cannot," he replied. "Then," said the boatman, "the WHOLE of your life is lost." It is to be hoped that the boatman, after the learned Professor had become fully sensible of the utility of a knowledge of the art of swimming, gave the necessary help to save his companion.

CHAPTER XII.

ARTIFICIAL AIDS TO SWIMMING.

  You cannot swim with floats, you know,
   With either style or grace ;
  Their proper use I'll try to show
   At the right time and place.

The use of mechanical contrivances as a means of acquiring the art of swimming should be avoided as far as possible. There are numerous inventions of this kind, such as cork floats, etc. The most venerable, and at the same time valueless, are the cork floats or buoys, something after the style of the old-fashioned life-preservers. The writer remembers a case which occurred to a shipmate who, being desirous of learning the art, had recourse to one of the ship's life-preservers to assist him in making for the shore ; but the float slipped from its place, and, losing all self-control, he sank head foremost—the life-preserver catching on his feet, effectually prevented him rising, and he would have perished had I not rescued him from his perilous position. With artificial aids a man can but be buoyed up. The art of swimming, when once acquired on correct principles, enables one to buoy himself, and move in any direction he wills instantaneously. This skill once acquired cannot be forgotten. The use of artificial aids, however good they may be, leaves less freedom of action to the body than is the case when they are dispensed with, and the learner who desires to swim with grace and ease is placed at a disadvantage by their use. Their use not only destroys the spirit of self-reliance, but actually fosters timidity, and leads to incapacity in case of emergency. Artificial aids have a tendency to tempt boys to venture beyond their depth before they can swim, and I do not think it possible to learn to swim successfully by their use. This brings us to the consideration of the aid afforded by a line, one end of which is secured around the chest of the learner, and the other being held by the teacher. A full description of this legitimate means of teaching this useful accomplishment will be found elsewhere.

CHAPTER XIII.

THE BUOYANCY OF WATER.

"These limbs that buoyant waves hath borne."—*Byron.*

It would be well for the novice to understand at the outset, that the water is in itself sufficiently buoyant to support the body with very little exertion. This can be readily proven by the following method: Take a coin or other bright object in your hand upon entering the water, then, wading out to the depth of the knee, drop the coin to the bottom and stoop down to recover it; then wade out in water breast-high, again drop the coin as before, then endeavor, in the same manner, to recover it, and it will be found much more difficult to reach bottom than might be anticipated. For the moment the body is bent the limbs will be forced to the surface, and it will require considerable exertion to reach the object at the bottom. This proves conclusively that the water has the power to support the body upon its surface with very little effort. Salt water is much more buoyant than fresh; the following simple illustration will prove the truth of this assertion. Take a pail of fresh water and place in it a large potato. The potato will instantly sink to the bottom, then put in a measure of salt and stir it up, whereupon the potato will rise to the surface and remain floating.

A swimmer who can cover seven miles in fresh water should be able to swim twenty-one miles in salt water with equal ease.

CHAPTER XIV.

THE NECESSITY OF CONFIDENCE.

"Confidence is the first essential to success."

The one indispensable requisite in learning the art of swimming is absolute confidence in the power of the water to support the human body upon its surface; this confidence once acquired, all the rest is comparatively easy. As swimming is considered the most necessary accomplishment of almost all out-door sports, every person should try to overcome any fear they may have entertained regarding the water, so as to take pleasure in its liquid depths. Some brave young fellows take to the water as naturally as a "duck," and are able to swim in from one to five lessons. Others keep shy of the water until the use and practice wears off the aversion. They have no confidence, and so they are retarded in acquiring the art, and it is this that tries the patience of the teacher—he has ten times more trouble with a timid youth than with a plucky one. These timid youths are the bane of a teacher's existence; they require the greatest care and attention in teaching. Every direction has to be repeated again and again, until the teacher's patience is well nigh exhausted. They should be treated with kindness and forbearance, for if an impatient word is uttered, or they are "ducked" or ill-used, they will go away discouraged, giving up all hope of the art. Every effort should be made by the teacher to enable them to overcome their timidity. Then only will they be able to receive instruction, and act upon it, for after they have acquired confidence they enjoy every attempt that brings them nearer perfection in this noble art. In direct contrast to these timid youths, are the courageous ones who plunge fearlessly into the water, obeying every direction given by the swimming master with alacrity. These brave youths are a positive boon to the teacher, inspiring him with the belief that his care and attention will be eventually rewarded; they are possessed of a strong desire to become good swimmers, and do all in their power to obtain a thorough knowledge of the art by paying strict attention to the orders of the teacher, and following them to the best of their ability.

These are the youths who, if properly handled, soon become good and successful swimmers, able to carry off a certificate in any swimming school. With such material a first-class swimming club can be established that will hold its own against all comers.

CHAPTER XV.

HOW TO ACQUIRE CONFIDENCE.

"Confidence once gained is easily retained."

In the writer's opinion, there can be nothing more calculated to put confidence into young and timid swimmers than the constant practising of the many different positions and ways of using the body and limbs in the water, for in swimming, as in everything else, "practice makes perfect." Man does not swim instinctively, but he can soon be taught to do so, and very little practice will give him confidence. Every novice should know that his body is specifically lighter than the water, and that it is almost impossible for the body to sink if left to itself. It is not necessary that the swimmer should remain long in the water, but simple practice for a short time every day will give him sufficient confidence to trust himself out of his depth. Confidence, then, being such a valuable adjunct in learning to swim, the pupil should industriously apply himself to the task with faithfulness. He should visit any public bath in his vicinity, but if there should not happen to be a building of this kind available, he should go to the nearest body of water that may be convenient; the result will amply repay him for his trouble and any expense he may incur in accomplishing his purpose. To learn how to swim means to learn how to save life in the water—how to take care of yourself and of others in case of disaster, as well as how to enjoy one of the most delightful exercises. Are not these, then, potent reasons for endeavoring to overcome all fear of the water and acquiring the necessary confidence, with the aid of which you will eventually become a successful swimmer? The foregoing remarks apply with equal force to ladies. Many of my own lady pupils have become expert swimmers.

CHAPTER XVI.

THE DANGER OF CRAMPS.

I have thought it best at the very outset to dispose of this fear-inspiring subject which, to many would-be swimmers, is a constant source of alarm, and I will endeavor to do so in as few words as possible. Cramp is simply a contraction of the muscles, usually produced by entering the water when the body is overheated, or remaining undressed upon the bank too long before entering the water. Either or both of these will produce cramp, though it may arise from other causes.

The Remedy for Cramps.

It is usually the arms or legs which are most subject to this complaint among swimmers. The most effectual remedy known is to turn on the back, throw the arm or kick the limb out of the water as vigorously as possible; this will cause a momentary pain as it straightens the contracted muscle. I have invariably found it produces the desired effect however, and the swimmer can proceed with the exercise. Above all things avoid getting excited, preserve your presence of mind, and you will be all right.

CHAPTER XVII.

DEFORMITY NO IMPEDIMENT TO ACQUIRING THE ART OF SWIMMING.

> "'If in the month of dark December
> Leander, who was nightly wont
> (What maid will not the tale remember?)
> To cross thy stream, broad Hellespont!"
> —*Byron.*

The world-renowned swimming feats of Lord Byron are confirmatory of the foregoing remarks. His famous swim across the Hellespont affords a striking instance of the power of will to overcome physical infirmities. A little of the sporting man's love of feats and "records" entered into the joy which Childe Harold felt in subduing the sea's white horses to his hand. It is a well-known fact that Byron was justly proud of his skill as a swimmer. Upon one occasion he challenged his friend and companion, Trelawney, to swim a long distance to a ship and to lunch in the water. The feat was successfully performed by both. This, and other similar feats, caused him to be styled the rival of Leander.

Lord Clandeboye, the eldest son of Canada's most popular Governor-General, Lord Dufferin, also swam across the Hellespont in the summer of 1883. One of the most expert swimmers on this continent is an American citizen named Cole, who, with only one arm, has frequently carried off the principal honors in many well-contested matches. Many persons who are helpless cripples on *terra firma* become extremely active in the watery element, frequently outstripping their more fortunate comrades who ashore would feel it an affliction to accommodate their vigorous strides to the cripples' labored locomotion.

There is another class of deformed persons who should not be overlooked, viz., those whose limbs are well-formed, but whose body is misshapen. The hunchback for instance, by reason of his deformity, would find it almost as difficult a matter to sink as the novice would to float. The malformation of his body increases his buoyancy to such an extent that it would be almost impossible for him to get his head beneath the waves. The author recalls the skill of an old schoolmate, a hunchback, who was one of the most daring and intrepid swimmers he ever knew; he would swim faster and venture out farther than many of his well-formed companions, who were considered expert in other branches of the art.

CHAPTER XVIII.

BREAST STROKE.

<blockquote>
See how the first-class swimmer swims,
  With steady stroke and true;
The graceful movements of his limbs
  A pattern for you.
</blockquote>

The beginner, having selected a proper bathing-place, should wade in up to his breast, turn round, face the shore, and take his preliminary "duck" by plunging head and shoulders under water, thus

Fig. 1.

Fig. 2.

preventing a rush of blood to the head; then rising, without hurrying or nervousness, bring the hands together with the palms downwards, thumbs and outer edges of the forefingers close together, and the hands slightly convexed at the back, and brought under the chin on a level with the shoulders, thumbs and forefingers of each hand being in contact; for in this way only are they a support from the time they start till they come back to the starting position. The elbows should be bent laterally on a level with the breast (Fig. 1), in order to secure the most effective stroke. The learner should then steadily incline his body forward, at the same time advancing his arms to their fullest extent, keeping the hands close together, just below the surface, neither elevating nor depressing the fingers—they should be kept at their full stretch for at least one second (Fig. 2). This

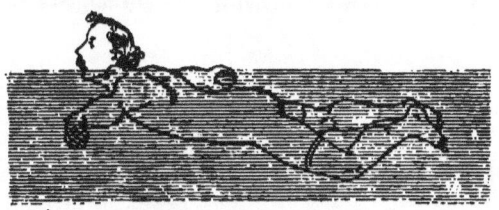

Fig. 3.

movement will bring his legs to the surface. He should then separate his hands and turn them back to back, still keeping the fingers close together, sweeping his arms obliquely backwards and downwards towards the body, drawing the legs up at the same time laterally, rather than under the body as in the old method (see Fig. 3). The elbows thus come back to the body, and the hands are brought quickly together as before to their first position under the chin, the edges only being presented to the water until the hands meet. At the same time the feet are brought together, as shown in Fig. 4. The arms should

Fig. 4.

then be shot forward, and the legs kicked out to their fullest extent, as shown in Fig. 5. The arms still retain their position, and the legs are brought together like a pair of scissors (as shown in Fig. 5a), which action will shoot the body forward like an arrow. Retain this position till the force of the stroke is exhausted. This method will send you ahead two or three yards at least. By paying particular attention to the foregoing directions, the pupil's hands will always be in advance of a line drawn through his shoulders—a necessary precaution to escape a ducking.

My reasons for advocating this method are the same as those which induced my old comrade, Edward Hanlan (for many years World's Champion Oarsman), to drop the short, jerky, fisherman's stroke, and adopt a long, sweeping stroke, in which every muscle of the body is

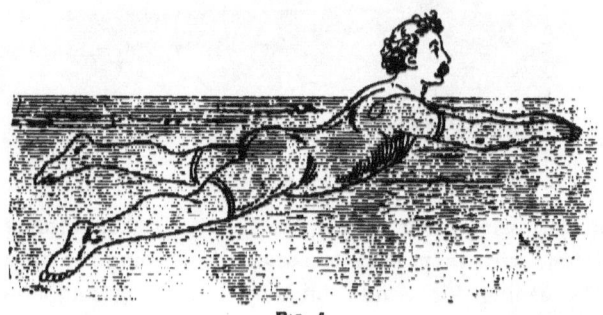

Fig. 5.

brought into play, thereby in the most graceful manner equalizing the muscular force necessary to send him to the front. His numerous victories amply prove the value of the change.

Fig. 5a.

CHAPTER XIX.

BREAST SWIMMING.

"And I have loved thee, Ocean! and my joy
Of youthful sports was on thy breast to be
Borne, like thy bubbles, onward; from a boy
I wanton'd with thy breakers—they, to me,
Were a delight; and if the freshening sea
Made them a terror—'twas a pleasing fear,
For I was, as it were, a child of thee,
And trusted to thy billows far and near,
And laid my hand upon thy mane—as I do here."
— *Byron*.

To show the value of breast swimming, the following account of a gallant rescue by a coast-guardsman, named George Oatley, may be interesting: "A few years ago, a Swedish vessel, named the *Augusta* of Uddawalla, was cast upon the rocks, and it seemed all hope of saving the crew was cut off; but the brave Oatley performed the daring feat of swimming through a blinding surf with a line to the vessel, and succeeded, by means of Manby's apparatus, in sending the crew on shore; not, however, until he was himself drawn ashore, was it known how very nearly his own life was to being sacrificed in his efforts to save them. On the recommendation of Admiral H. R. H. the Duke of Edinburgh, the Queen conferred on Oatley the well-earned distinction of the Albert Medal of the first class. The Queen performed the ceremony of presenting the medal herself, alighting from her carriage on a journey from Windsor to Balmoral at a place called Ferryhill Junction, where a platform was erected, and Her Majesty pinned the decoration on the breast of the brave man in the presence of a crowd of spectators."

The Swedish Government also conferred decorations on the man, besides a number of Humane Societies.

CHAPTER XX.

SWIMMING ON THE BACK.

This accomplishment is very easy to acquire, and not only most useful, but may be said to be indispensable to those who have to swim long distances, or remain for a considerable time in the water, as it can be performed with greater ease than any other method.

While swimming on the breast, as described in the previous chapter, you can turn on your back in the deepest water, by throwing up the left hand out of the water, and pressing the right downwards in the water, this will turn you completely over instantly; then allow the head to fall back until the water is level with the ears, this will bring the face and chest above the surface of the water; then place your arms "akimbo" with the palms resting on your hips, and draw your knees up laterally at right angles with the body, bringing the feet close together (see Fig. 6), then kick the legs

FIG. 6.

out to their fullest extent (see Fig. 7), bring them together quickly, as

FIG. 7.

shown in the breast stroke (see Fig. 8), allowing yourself to shoot

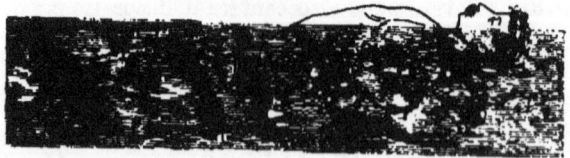

FIG. 8.

ahead until the force of the effort is exhausted. You can vary the movement of the arms, by throwing them forward with the hands held "concave" like a spoon-shaped oar, sweeping them down toward the

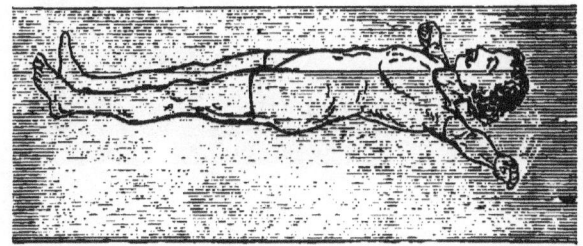

Fig. 9.

side with a semi-circular motion (see Fig. 9), or you may hold one or both arms perfectly upright out of the water at pleasure. In orna-

Fig. 10.

mental swimming some contestants hold flags in their hands, and swim in this manner over the entire course (see Fig. 10.)

Fig. 11.

Again you can fold your arms across the chest, *à la Napoleon* (see Fig. 11), or behind your back, if so disposed; this will give the chest an additional elevation of two or three inches above the water

Fig. 12.

(see Fig. 12); or you may stretch the hands straight in advance of the head, locking the thumbs together (see Fig. 13).

Fig. 13.

In addition to these methods you can add another, by keeping the hands straight before the head, but widely apart (see Fig. 14); or you

Fig. 14.

may clasp them behind the head, with the elbows at right angles, continuing the progressive movement (see Fig. 15).

Fig. 15.

CHAPTER XXI.

SIDE STROKE.

This stroke is generally learned after the common breast stroke has been acquired. It is the swiftest means of propulsion through the water that can be adopted, and is specially of service in competitions as to speed.

In what is known as a "go-as-you-please" contest, where each competitor has the privilege of swimming in any manner he may choose, the person adopting this stroke, other things being equal, has a great advantage, it being easier and more effective than the breast stroke. Side swimming is usually said to be more exhausting than breast swimming. This is, however, a matter of opinion. Captain Webb, in his celebrated swim across the English Channel, swam the whole distance, about twenty-three miles, on his breast. Horace Davenport, E. T. Jones, Willie Beckwith, Thomas Finney, and others, have accomplished considerable distances on the side. From the writer's own knowledge, he concludes that, for long, enduring display, the breast stroke is preferable; while in races where speed is wanted the side stroke is best, in fact, it is unequalled. There is a diversity of opinion as to the position which should be adopted by the side swimmer; some advocate the right as best, and nearly all self-taught swimmers lie on the right side in executing this stroke. The author prefers the left, for the following reasons: The upper arm, in the side stroke, is the one which has the most work to do; it is better, therefore, to place the stronger arm (generally the right) in that position.

It is admitted that the strain upon the chest is considerable in breast swimming, while it is rarely felt in side swimming. There is, however, one drawback in connection with the side stroke, and that is "steering." In breast swimming the human body is symmetrically situated, and the propelling force being equal at both sides, the body advances in a straight line ahead, and the steering is easy. In side swimming greater care is required; the learner must understand that the head is the helm, the slightest inclination of which will alter the course, and as it is awkward to look ahead in this position, he had better align two fixed objects in the rear and steer by them. This is the only drawback, if it be one, to the side stroke. Its advantages are many. The best method of effecting this stroke is as follows:

The learner should lie upon the left side, stretching out the left arm to its fullest extent in advance of his head, the right arm should be straightened out in the opposite direction, so that the palm of the hand rests upon the right hip. The legs should be stretched out at full length and kept close together, with the feet turned back in such a manner that the toes are in a direct line with the knees, as shown in Fig. 16.

Fig. 16.

In executing the first arm stroke, the left arm should be struck downwards and backwards, that is, toward the body, and then brought up under the head by bending the elbow, while the right arm is brought under the level of the chin as far beyond the head as can be managed without lowering the right shoulder, so that the elbow of the right arm will just lie over the fingers of the left hand (see Fig. 17).

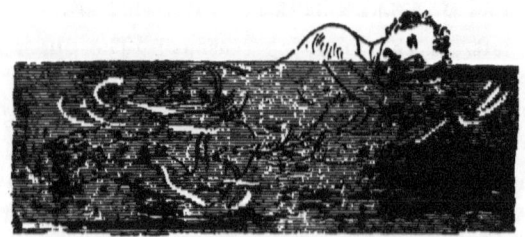

Fig. 17.

Care should be taken to glide the right hand along below the surface, and in such a manner as to offer the least possible resistance to the water.

In making the first leg stroke the knees should be drawn up gently until the thighs form a right angle with the body. The feet being kept close together and the knees wide apart, as shown in Fig. 17. The first leg stroke and the first arm stroke should be executed at the same time. The second leg stroke is made by extending the right leg in a line with the thigh of the same leg, at right angles with the body, and then straightening the left thigh in a direct line with the body, and bending the same leg at the knee backwards, so as to enclose between both the legs and thighs as large a body of water as possible (see Fig. 18). In executing the third leg stroke,

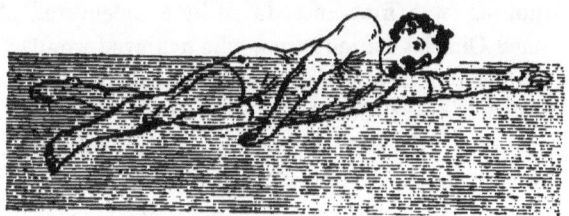

Fig. 18.

the thighs and legs should be brought together with considerable energy, the left leg coming forward with a flat-like motion, and the right leg falling back till they meet in their original position (Fig. 16).

Simultaneously with the second and third leg strokes, the second arm stroke should be executed. In order to make the second arm stroke effective it is absolutely necessary that the right hand, which is in advance of the head, should be hollowed, knuckles uppermost, with the thumb and fingers firmly pressed together. The hand should then be sharply pulled back toward the body and close to the chest, till it regains its former position on the right hip. The left hand, meantime, extended to its original position in advance of the head (see Fig. 16). This completes the five movements, three for the legs, and two for the arms, required for the correct performance of the side stroke.

The action of the right arm in its forward motion may be varied; by raising the arm clear of the water, and then reaching forward as far as possible, then dipping the hand, as in the Indian stroke, (see Fig. 19), and although this is not, strictly speaking, the correct style

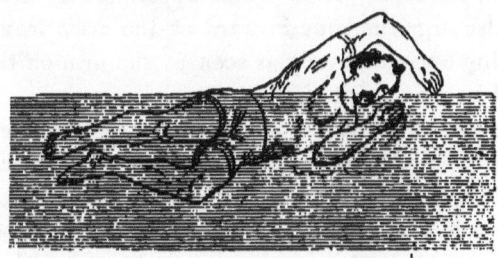

Fig. 19.

to adopt by any person desirous of becoming a graceful swimmer, this will be found most useful in speed contests. One of the most popular exponents of the side stroke is Mr. Horace Davenport, the Amateur Champion Swimmer of Great Britain, whom the author had the pleasure of meeting while in Canada in the summer of 1882. This style of swimming was first introduced by a celebrated Australian swimmer named Charles Saundstrum, who achieved wonderful success as a side swimmer. I have endeavored, as far as possible, to describe from memory the exact detail of his method. Several American swimmers, including Ernest Von Schœning, George H. Wade, Wm. H. Daly, Tony Butler, and George Hyslop (of Hamilton, Canada), have achieved considerable notoriety as "side stroke" swimmers. Captain J. L. Rawbone, R. H. S., of the Dolphin Swimming Club, Toronto, has also won a number of gold and silver medals by his skill in this style of swimming; in 1887 he won the championship of Toronto Bay from W. B. Swain, formerly champion of Tunbridge Wells, England. He also holds the Royal Humane Society's bronze medal for saving life July 27th, 1883.

CHAPTER XXII.
"HAND OVER HAND."

In this popular mode of swimming, one arm should be raised above the surface and thrust forward to its fullest extent, the other hand at the same time describing a small curve in a downward direction, to maintain the balance of the body. The advanced hand is to be slightly hollowed as it enters the water, which it grasps and pulls as it were diagonally to the opposite arm-pit, while the other, in a widely described arc, is to be passed quickly under the breast in the direction of the hips. Each arm is uppermost in turn.

The legs also urge the body forward as the arms leave the water, each leg striking out alternately as soon as the arm on the same side has completed its movement.

The whole movement of the arm describes an oval figure, of which the lower part is *in*, and the other *out*, of the water, while the shoulder forms the centre after being thrown forward; the hand is turned as it touches the water, so that it encounters little resistance on entering the water, but it is immediately turned with the knuckle upward and the palm hollowed out as in "side swimming."

Fig. 20 shows the body just as the right arm has finished its circular sweep, and the left is beginning to rise.

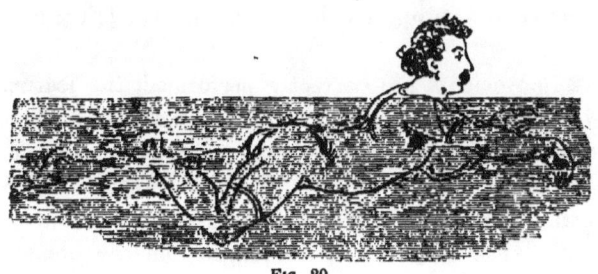

Fig. 20.

During these movements the swimmer appears to be hurled forward by the swing of the arms, and makes considerable progress as to distance, but the method is too fatiguing to be adopted for any length of time. It is very useful as a relief from the ordinary mode.

CHAPTER XXIII.

THE DOG STROKE.

This movement is similar to a dog or horse when trotting—that is, the right arm and left leg make one stroke, say a negative or forward movement, while the left arm and right leg make the other, or a positive stroke backward; so the two limbs taken crosswise are making the propelling stroke, while the other two, of course crosswise, as well, are making the retarding stroke. This diagonal and similar action keeps the body at the same level and the speed uniform (see Fig. 21). To do this the learner should wade into the water till

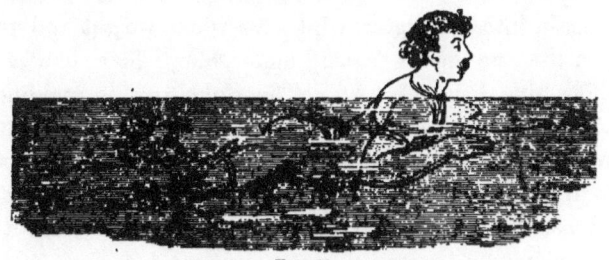

Fig. 21.

it reaches the arm-pits, then imitate with his hands the action of a dog's fore-paws when swimming, at the same time raising the legs to a nearly horizontal position, while beating the water down and back, first with the right arm and left leg, then with the left arm and right leg.

If these movements are correctly performed, the learner cannot fail to swim, providing he takes care *always* to keep his hands in advance of his shoulders ; neglect of this will lead to a loss of balance, and his head will undoubtedly become immersed. The Sclavonic tribes, Russians, Poles, Laplanders, etc., usually swim in a manner somewhat similar to this, and as a change from the breast-stroke it will be found useful. It is also an easy method for a learner to acquire, as the exertion necessary is very little, and of the simplest kind. Quadrupeds instinctively adopt this method, and as man, until he becomes expert, has to imitate them in using all four limbs for support and propulsion in the water, this mode is at least as natural as any other for beginners.

CHAPTER XXIV.

THE INDIAN STROKE.

The mode of swimming in use among the Indian tribes in Canada and the United States is as peculiar as their manner of walking.

The stroke used by the various tribes in North America is quite different from that usually practised in the civilized world.

The Indian, instead of parting his hands simultaneously in front of the head, and making the stroke outward in a nearly horizontal direction, thus causing a rather severe strain upon the chest, throws his body forward alternately upon the right and left side, raising one arm entirely out of the water, and reaching as far forward as possible to dip it again into the water, whilst his whole weight and force are spent upon the one that is passing under him, which, like a paddle, is propelling him along (Fig. 22). The right arm is making a half circle, and is being raised out of the water behind him, the opposite arm being raised above his head, describing a similar arc in the air, to be again dipped into the water as far as he can reach before him, the hand bent inwards so as to form a sort of cup, and thus act most effectively as it passes in its turn beneath him.

In this bold and powerful mode of swimming, which may certainly be deficient in the grace that many wish to see, there is little strain upon the breast and spine. This mode enables the swimmer to get

Fig. 22.

through the water more speedily than the breast stroke does. It is, however, less rapid than the side stroke, and more fatiguing than either the breast or side stroke.

CHAPTER XXV.

FLOATING.

The ability to float is one of the first essentials in swimming. When long distances have to be accomplished, a tired swimmer is enabled by this means to rest his exhausted frame until he gains sufficient strength to pursue his course. Persons float with much greater ease in salt water than they do in fresh. Women float much easier than men, the principal reason of this being that their bones are lighter, and their adipose tissue much greater than that of men. For the same reason fat persons float naturally. I remember a case of one very corpulent old gentleman whom I was endeavoring to teach to swim on his back, who found it almost as difficult to turn over as a mud-turtle when laid in the same position. Some of my lady pupils could float for ten or fifteen minutes consecutively. There are two styles of floating, viz., the horizontal and the perpendicular.

Horizontal Floating.

Stretch yourself out at full length on your back, holding the arms close to the side. In this position the toes, the upper part of the chest and the face, will appear above the surface of the water (see Fig. 23). At each inspiration the body will rise an inch or an inch and

FIG. 23.

a half, and at each respiration it will sink about the same depth. A slight movement of the hands, palms downwards, the arms being held close to the sides, so slight as to seem almost imperceptible to the onlooker, is quite sufficient to maintain this position. Some experts can even fold the arms across the chest, and float with comparative ease.

Perpendicular Floating.

Assume an upright position in the water. Extend the arms at right angles with the body, palms downward; stretch forward the right leg, and beating the water with the hands to maintain an equilibrium (see Fig. 24), one can float in this manner for a considerable length of time. By throwing the head back until the water is level with the ears, as shown in Fig. 25, you can float much more easily. To persons who cannot swim, this will be found particularly valuable should they, by any unforeseen accident, find themselves in the water. By considering this carefully in time of security, they will be enabled to act upon it in time of danger.

CHAPTER XXVI.

TREADING WATER.

Treading water is accomplished by allowing the feet to fall from a floating or swimming position, and performing with the legs the same motion that is made in going up a flight of stairs. This method has the advantage of sustaining the body at a uniform height. The feat is more easily achieved when the arms are employed to assist the legs, by pressing the water with a downward motion, (as shown in Fig. 25.)

Expert swimmers, however, prefer to depend entirely on the legs for support, and either fold the arms across the breast, hold them high above the head, or extend them horizontally along the surface of the water, with some article in each hand.

Fig. 24.

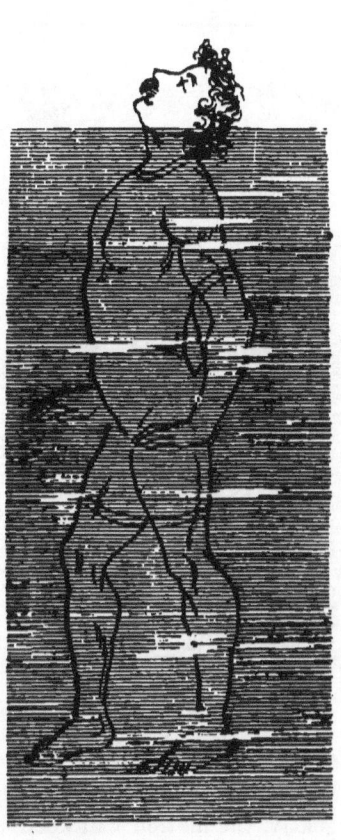

Fig. 25.

Williams, the celebrated swimmer from the Island of Malta, at the annual tournament held by the Montreal Swimming Club some years ago, performed the clever feat of holding two small flags in each hand extended at arms length, and balancing a bottle of champagne on his head while treading water; he also dined in the water. This I have endeavored to duplicate (see Figs. 26, 27).

Treading water is specially useful in the event of a person who, while heavily clothed, falls accidentally into the water, as it is the very best position that can be assumed in the water to enable the person to remove impeding garments; and if a person, being unable to swim, should fall overboard, or from a wharf or pier, or otherwise accidentally find himself so exposed to danger, by preserving coolness,

Fig. 26.

Fig. 27.

and in this way having recourse to treading water—placing his arms horizontally slightly below the surface, and keeping them moving gently, the motion will keep him safe till help arrives.

By extending one foot before the other, and allowing the head to fall back till the water is level with the ears, he can float securely for a considerable length of time, as already shown (Fig. 24).

CHAPTER XXVII.

JUMPING INTO THE WATER.

This method of entering the water will be found especially serviceable to those who cannot swim, in cases of shipwreck, or the burning of a vessel, or during a collision, where the watery element seems to offer a better chance of escape than to remain on board of the ill-fated vessel. The jump may be made in the following manner: Take a full breath, and then spring forward as far as possible, to clear the ship, so as to avoid being engulfed in the vortex which the sinking ship will make. Keep the body straight until it is submerged; the feet and limbs held firmly together. (Fig. 28.)

The arms have to be extended above the head, with the fingers locked together, so as to ensure the arms being kept in position. If the leap is taken from a considerable height, as, for instance, the promenade deck of a steamer, and the body should deviate from the perpendicular, it may be rectified by inclining the head and arms in the opposite direction, taking care, however, to have them vertical at the instant of entering the water. When the swimmer wishes to stop his descent, after entering the water, all he has to do is to spread his arms, and he will at once commence to rise.

Fig. 28.

A number of foolhardy persons, such as Donovan, who leaped from the Suspension Bridge into the Hudson River, which is probably one of the highest jumps on record, have achieved considerable notoriety by their unjustifiable desire for fame.

CHAPTER XXVIII.

PLUNGING.

> "And with his harness on his back,
> Plunged headlong in the tide."
> —Macaulay, "*Lays of Ancient Rome.*"

Plunging is the act of springing into the water head-first. This is the only method of entering the water which a dashing swimmer will allow himself to use; when the learner has become somewhat familiar with the element and its buoyant power, and has learned the proper use of his limbs in it, according to the instructions contained in the previous pages of this work, he will look with some degree of contempt upon walking into the water after the very mild manner that is only appropriate to those who cannot swim. He will not be satisfied until he is able to throw a little more spirit into the proceedings, and enter the water with a plunge; and, in learning to do so, he must practise with as much care and attention as he displayed in the previous lessons. The progress should be quite gradual, until the learner is able to plunge, with perfect confidence, from a height of twenty-five feet, or more. So accurately can this be done, that it is a well-known practice among expert swimmers to mount a tree or other elevation, throw a wooden hoop into the water, and dive through it without touching its sides. These remarks apply with equal force to ladies. Many of my female pupils attained great proficiency in the art of plunging and diving.

Fig. 29.

The author would impress upon the learner the importance of ascertaining the depth of the water before plunging into it; for while it is important that the water should not be too deep (even although the swimmer may have learned the rudiments of swimming), it is far more important that it should not be too shallow. Great care must, therefore, be taken to avoid both extremes.

In learning to plunge, the palms of the hands should be placed together and the arms extended in advance of the head, so as to present a wedge, by which the water is separated to admit the passage of the head through its substance. There is sometimes a nervousness with learners in beginning to plunge, as if the water would hurt like a hard substance; this fear can be got rid of by the learner assuming the attitude shown in Fig. 29, and tumble himself forward, thus gaining confidence. One good "header" that occupies but a moment or two, will prevent chills, headaches and other unpleasant sensations that usually follow the objectionable plan of wading into the water by inches.

There are cases where a swimmer is obliged to enter the water where it is not of sufficient depth to permit the ordinary plunge; the best way is to make a run forward and throw the body nearly, but not quite, horizontally into the water, and to curve the back as far as possible, when the head has fairly touched the surface (see Fig. 30).

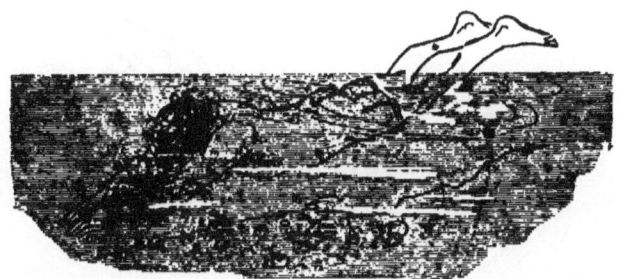

Fig. 30.

This style is adopted by the Eton College boys, and is generally known as the Eton plunge. An expert will boldly throw himself into the water in this manner from the bank, although only three feet or so in depth. Indeed, there are some who can manage this feat so adroitly, that their heads actually emerge above the surface as their feet are submerged.

Great care must be taken to hold the body firmly braced, as the sudden change of curve in the spine is apt to cause a strain that might lead to dangerous results.

When executed properly the head dips but little below the surface, the back is just covered, and the whole figure slanted upwards again immediately.

The Low Plunge.

Frequent practice of this most useful feat is strongly recommended. When made from a height of say four or five feet, the body should be bent down until the head is lower than the knees, which should be opened to allow the head and arms a free passage. The arms should be extended, as already shown, in front of the head, the hands joined to cleave a passage through the water. The learner should then gradually incline forward till he loses his balance, and then at once straighten the body from the fingers to the toes. If the directions have been strictly followed, the learner enters the water hands first, and as noiselessly as an arrow.

The Popular Plunge.

Another method of accomplishing the same thing, is to take a slight spring from the platform, and immediately that the body is in the air, to straighten it then and enter the water diagonally, body

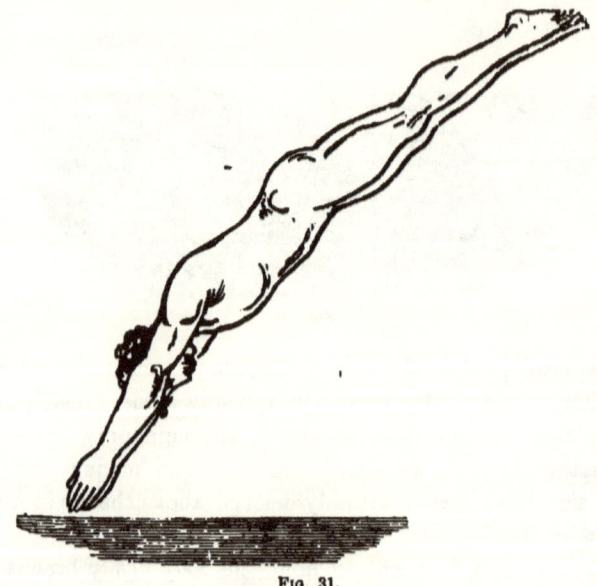

FIG. 31.

straight and rigid, head downwards, the heels close together, and hands extended in advance of the head, and in a line with the body (see Fig. 31). This mode exhibits more grace, but requires skill on the part of the swimmer to execute it properly.

The High Plunge.

When the high plunge is taken from a height of ten or fifteen feet, it is advisable to spring forward, so that the body may not strike the water perpendicularly.

This precaution will greatly mitigate the effects of the concussion felt at the instant of contact, because by this method the resistance is progressively surmounted; but for any height much in excess of fifteen feet, the forward spring is useless as a means of giving obliquity to the line of descent, though it may be useful to enable a swimmer to clear any intervening obstacle that may be between the height from which he plunges and the surface of the water, such as the side of a vessel for instance.

There is one thing specially to be avoided in order to make this plunge successful, and that is, throwing up the heels after the feet have left the platform in making the spring, as the doing so will impart an extra rotary motion to the body, and thus render it a matter of uncertainty which part will first touch the water. Any deviation from the correct attitude will be detected, and entail immediate punishment, more or less severe, according to the height of the plunge, the part of the body that is out of position, and the extent of the error.

If the learner takes a long flat board, and first lets it drop endways from a height of ten or fifteen feet into the water, and afterwards lets it fall from the same height on the flat, the great resistance which the water will offer to it in the latter case compared to the former, will show how important it is that the correct posture should be learned before plunging from any considerable height. By constant practice the novice soon gains the requisite presence of mind which enables him to leap from any height without feeling at all disconcerted.

Many of my pupils, including a number of ladies, were able to accomplish the high plunge successfully.

Many persons take great delight in performing feats of daring, as they are pleased to term them. Seamen especially have a fondness for achievements of this nature.

Many stories are related of great plunging feats from the masthead of vessels. Among them I select the following, which may prove interesting

A seaman, belonging to H.M.S. *Canada*, plunged from the mast-head into the sea, a distance of over one hundred feet, going down on the port side, passing under the vessel's keel, and coming up on the starboard side, some distance from the vessel, to which he swam below the surface, and supporting himself by the rudder chains under the counter for a considerable time, until it was thought he was hopelessly lost; he then swam to the ship's side, to the great delight of the officers and crew.

Mr. John D. Patry, of the Dolphin Swimming Club, Toronto, has also distinguished himself as an expert in this branch of aquatic performances, by winning the Andrews' Silver Medal for 1882, 1883 and 1884. He also accompanied the author in the life-boat to the rescue of Professor Schlochow, during the terrible gale of July 27th, 1883, for which he received the Bronze Medal of the Royal Humane Society.

CHAPTER XXIX.

THE "HEADER."

The genuine "header" may be taken either from the bank with a run or from a height. It is better to learn both ways, and, indeed, every way by which the human body can be transferred from the land to the water. To take a proper "header," the hands should be joined over the head and the arms extended in front at full length, in order to cleave a passage for the head before it reaches the water. If this precaution be not taken, the top of the head gets a terrible blow in the contact with the surface. The back should be well-hollowed, the entire body as stiff as a poker, the legs stretched at full length and firmly held together, the feet being closely pressed to each other and the toes well-pointed so as to offer as little resistance as possible to the water. Considerable practice is necessary in order to become proficient in this most useful acquirement.

The test of a perfect "header" is that it raises no splash, and the body seems to slide into the water like a beaver or an otter, merely leaving a series of concentric circles and bubbling spots in their centre to mark the spot where the plunger disappeared from view. Among the greatest authenticated distances attained in plunging, was that accomplished by R. Green, Margaret Street Baths, Liverpool, Eng., in July 17th, 1879, when he succeeded in plunging 68 feet 4 inches. Horace Davenport, at Lambeth Baths, London, Eng., in October, 1878, went 62 feet 7 inches, and in August, 1880, he got a distance of 58 feet 8 inches in open water at Norwood, England.

The Running Header.

This feat is accomplished by running ten or twelve paces before springing into the water, the order of the steps being so arranged that the last one is made by the foot with which it is intended to execute the spring, the swimmer's aim being to endeavor to clear as great a distance as possible before touching the water. Muscular strength and lightness of the body are the main requisites for the successful accomplishment of this popular method of plunging. Another wrinkle worth knowing is, that by curving the body and limbs so as to make them coincide with the line of transit, that is the trajectory, this will be found a great aid—in fact, must be done to insure an undisturbed cleavage of the water, as already shown.

In all other respects the instructions already given under the "Header" will apply.

The Skimming Plunge.

This method of plunging is more difficult to acquire than the previous one; but, when thoroughly mastered, it will be found one of the most useful, as it certainly is one of the most graceful, feats in swimming. In fact, a person's ability as a swimmer may be pretty accurately determined by the way in which he plunges, even before he swims a stroke.

FIG. 32.

This style of plunging is of the greatest service in water that is shallow, or of which the depth is unknown, also when the swimmer desires that the impetus of the spring should aid his progress, as in a swimming match, or when there is a necessity for reaching any object in a short time, as, for example, when a fellow-creature is in danger of drowning.

It consists in springing forward, and, directly the feet leave the ground, straightening the body and making it perfectly rigid. The arms are to be extended in advance of the head, the forefingers of each hand to be in contact, and the palms to be held either downward or close together.

The thighs and legs, from the hips to the big toes, are to be kept close, and the feet turned back until the insteps of both feet are in nearly a straight line with the shins, as shown in Fig. 32.

The body should still be held firm while moving along the surface, and the breath has, of course, to be held, if the face is kept downward. Some expert swimmers prefer turning the face upward, and gliding into the water on their back. This is certainly the most pleasant method of taking this plunge. The more closely the figure, entrance, and motion resemble that of an arrow discharged from a bow, the more graceful and effective is the plunge.

A distance of forty or fifty feet has been often accomplished by this method.

CHAPTER XXX.

SWIMMING UNDER WATER.

This style of swimming may be found useful, especially when performing such games as "Hunt the Duck," etc. It is frequently made a part of a swimming tournament as a test of the lung power of the contestants.

At the annual races of the Dolphin Swimming Club, a silver medal was awarded each year for this style of swimming. The contestants entered the water in the manner described under the head of the Skimming Plunge. Keeping so close to the surface, without breaking it, however, that they can be seen by the spectators for the entire distance, using only the breast stroke.

Long distances have been accomplished in this way. Mr. Alfred Potter, of the Dolphin Swimming Club, won the silver medal awarded by the Toronto Swimming Club, August, 1883, reaching the very creditable distance of 104 ft. In September, 1883, at the Dolphin Club Races, he exceeded this record by reaching 110 ft., receiving the Andrews' Medal therefor. Mr. Potter is the holder of a number of medals for diving, running, etc.

CHAPTER XXXI.

DIVING.

> 'Twas surely Providence who gave
> Our divers nerve so brave,
> To plunge beneath the stormy wave
> A human life to save.

Diving is the most exhilarating enjoyment to which a swimmer can attain. The ability to dive successfully is the ambition of every novice. He feels a certain amount of exultation in his power to descend beneath the surface, either for pleasure or to recover lost articles, or, if need be, save the life of one who has sunk and is in danger of drowning.

The primary essentials in diving are courage, and the lung capacity for retaining sufficient air to enable one to remain under water for a considerable time. Courage is an inherent virtue with many, but timidity may be overcome by constant practice. The usual length of time men can generally remain under water is about one minute. This time may be prolonged to a minute and a half or two minutes by the following method, which the author has found very successful. Prior to entering the water, the lungs should be inflated to their fullest capacity by taking in great draughts of pure air, retaining the breath as long as possible, then allow the air to escape, until the lungs become quite empty, continuing this practice until all the foul air has been discharged. This method will give you one-third more lung capacity than you would otherwise possess. Then take one large, full inspiration and dive into the water. The correct position for diving is that shown in Fig. 31, ch. xxviii. (see also illustration of ladies diving). The dive may be made either from a bank, vessel, or platform, and if the impetus given is not sufficient to enable him to reach the point aimed at, he can strike out with his limbs as in the breast stroke, until he reaches the object, precisely the same as if it were a floating one.

The objective point having been obtained, the swimmer should assume an upright position, pressing his feet firmly against the bottom, spring upward toward the surface, aiding himself in his ascent by using his arms and legs vigorously. Rapid movements underneath the water soon exhaust the quantity of air contained in the lungs,

Ladies Diving.

whereas if the person keeps perfectly still, he can remain below for a much longer period. On one occasion Professor Blatt (whom the author met in 1882) remained under water in a glass tank, at a public exhibition in Rochester, New York, for the extraordinary space of four minutes eleven and three-quarter seconds. On this occasion he assumed a sitting posture at the bottom of the tank, distinctly visible to the spectators through its glass sides; after a time his eyes closed, his head drooped forward on his chest, and his body rolled to one side in such a manner that the people became alarmed and insisted on his being taken out of the tank. This was instantly done, but it took some time to restore the Professor to consciousness. When able to stand upright, he staggered forward to the front of the platform and addressing the audience in a spirit of bravado, said, "Ladies and gentlemen, I can beat that." Professor Blatt had great lung capacity, and with his lady companion, who also possessed great lung power, performed many interesting feats in their glass tank beneath the surface of the water, such as sewing, calculating sums on a slate, the figures being called out by the audience, and other curious feats. Willie and Agnes Beckwith, of London, England, with whom I became personally acquainted during their stay in Toronto, also performed many extraordinary feats in a large glass tank at the Toronto Industrial Exhibition in 1883. The pearl and sponge divers of Ceylon cannot remain below the surface longer than two or three minutes, expert divers though they be, owing to the fact that in obtaining these articles the body is kept constantly in motion, thus exhausting their stock of air, and compelling them to return to the surface for a fresh supply.

The proper method is to enter the water with closed eyes, this, however, you will do naturally, but when beneath the surface they should be opened in order to see where you are going. The range of vision is necessarily limited under the water, and varies greatly with its purity or otherwise. In the clear, fresh water of our great Canadian lakes, especially Lake Superior, the waters of which are celebrated for their purity, objects can be discerned with wonderful clearness for many fathoms beneath the surface. This fact is so well known, that passengers on our palace steamers frequently throw small silver coin into the water for the pleasure of seeing the skill and dexterity displayed by some of the Indians in recovering them.

A remarkable case of rescue under the most trying circumstances, which could only have been successful by plucky diving, is worthy of record here.

In December, 1867, the French ship, *Nouveau Caboteur*, was cast ashore in the Bay of Zurriola, on the north coast of Spain, during a gale of wind; the sea at the time was running so heavily that no boat would venture to put off. There was also a general belief that it was impossible for a boat to be of any service.

At this crisis the British Vice-Consul of San Sebastian, Mr. E. B. March, after unsuccessfully entreating some of the bystanders to accompany him, plunged into the sea, swam to the vessel, and succeeded in bringing a rope to land. The rope was then secured, and one of the crew came ashore safely; the second (a lad) lost his hold, dropped into the sea, and sank. Mr. March, though benumbed with cold, at the greatest personal risk, again swam to the vessel, dived under her keel, recovered the lad, and brought him to land. The remainder of the crew (which consisted of six men in all), got safely to land.

Mr. March was for a time completely prostrated from the effects of his exertions and the intense cold, but by care and attention he was restored, a result scarcely to have been expected under the circumstances.

For this highly meritorious act of bravery, Mr. March received the Royal Humane Society's Medal and the Albert Medal of the first class.

CHAPTER XXXII.

SWIMMING IN CLOTHES.

Swimming in clothes will greatly tend
To make you strong and brave,
So that you may assistance lend
Another's life to save.

This is the highest grade of swimming, and should be encouraged by all swimming masters. The Royal Humane Society of England have recently issued a silver medallion, to be awarded to those skilled in this branch of the art, with a view to the greater preservation of life from drowning. The Dolphin Swimming Club have also awarded a number of silver medals with the same object in view. Sergeant Arthur E. Price, of the Royal Grenadiers, a hero of Batoche, who holds the silver medal and clasp for that campaign, has also won the Andrews' Silver Medals for 1883 and 1884, and the Wiman Silver Medal for 1885, for his proficiency in this difficult style of swimming.

It is particularly necessary where contests of this kind are held that the clothing to be worn should be clearly specified, in order that no contestant should gain an unfair advantage over his fellows.

This method is also valuable when it is necessary to jump into the water to save a fellow-creature from drowning.

Either the breast or side-stroke may be used at pleasure.

CHAPTER XXXIII.

UPRIGHT SWIMMING.

The upright position in swimming is recommended by some writers because in the "breast stroke" the head has to be bent back in order to raise the mouth and chin clear of the surface, and pain in the back of the neck is sometimes the consequence, especially if the swimmer is long in the water. This difficulty can be met by the swimmer changing position as the pain comes on.

In the "side stroke" the swimmer has only to incline the head toward the right or left shoulder, according to the side on which he prefers to swim, and thus the exercise may be greatly prolonged.

Some persons think that because mankind adopts the upright position in walking and running, they should swim in the same position. Those who advocate this method should remember that the greater the angle made by the legs the less the effective power, and that with an increase of depth there follows a proportionate increase of pressure, and consequently the more labor has to be expended, with but little progress compared with any other style of swimming.

Signor Oronzio de Bernardi, Professor of Swimming in the Naval Academy at Naples, Italy, is a strong believer in the upright position in swimming, going so far as to say that a good swimmer ought to make three miles an hour in this way. The writer does not think it possible, unless the wind and current come to the assistance of the swimmer; but under any circumstance the labor incurred in this method renders it undesirable except for very short distances, or simply as an exercise in ornamental swimming.

The upright, or perpendicular, swimming is practised by the natives of the East Indies, who swim out to meet vessels nearing their shores, to secure employment in discharging cargo. They usually swim in the track of the vessels until picked up; and, as they live on islands a distance from the mainland, on the vessel's return trip when nearing their homes, they drop into the water with their wages, in "kind," on their backs, and make for land; and although the distance is considerable sometimes, and the current strong, their skill in swimming, acquired from childhood, and their bravery, soon lands them safely at home. Having loads on their backs, they swim nearly upright, but when rid of their burden they revert to the horizontal position.

The French and German military schools teach upright swimming, beginning with perpendicular floating (see Fig. 24); next they instruct the learners to use their limbs as in walking, stretching the arms on either side, and putting one leg before the other so as to balance the body; simultaneously he gives a circular sweep with his arms on the water, striking the legs downward and forward, and when proficiency is acquired, he is able to perform the same motions in military drill perpendicularly in the water, that he generally executes vertically on land.

CHAPTER XXXIV.

FRENCH SWIMMING DRILL.

"Savoir nager est très utile pour un soldat."—*Andrews*.

The citizens of the great French Republic bestow a great deal of attention upon swimming, and, as a natural consequence, the French excel in the art. This is especially the case in the army and navy, no French soldier or sailor being considered *au fait* until he has obtained his certificate as a good swimmer. The art is taught upon purely scientific principles, namely, General Pfuest's system. The bathing establishments are built and the swimming masters appointed by the Government, and every citizen can obtain a sound practical knowledge of this useful accomplishment by visiting one of these establishments, which are to be found in every town and city of France, and the people are not slow to avail themselves of the opportunity so afforded them, some of them becoming splendid swimmers. As an example for our Canadian volunteers to follow, the author records the following interesting account (extracted from the *Penny Magazine*) of a remarkable swimming tournament, which took place in the River Seine, Paris, France, which indicates the high standard of excellence attained by French soldiers. It was, in fact, a test of what might be accomplished in an emergency. The first person to arrive was Viscount Courtioron, who left the swimming school in a boat containing thirteen men, and when he had reached the Quai d'Orsay, he leaped into the water, dressed and fully equipped as an infantry soldier, with accoutrements on; assuming the upright position, as described before, he raised himself out of the water at a distance of thirty fathoms, and discharged his rifle, which contained a heavy charge, and made a very loud report; at this signal, an old soldier who was stationed at Point Royal, leaped into the river from a bridge, the height being sixty-four feet, and swimming to the front, carried to M. Courtioron a tin box containing despatches, who after reading them, swam to the boat to give instructions to his men. Instantly sixty-five persons who had come with the colonel of the regiment in other boats, leaped into the water and followed his movements as if on parade, the orders being given by sound of trumpet, and in this way the evolutions were carried out successfully. The cavalry, mounted, are also exercised in swimming, so that in case of war, by this means an enemy may be surprised, or comrades rescued, or they may thus save themselves.

CHAPTER XXXV.

GERMAN SWIMMING SCHOOLS.

"Schwimmen zu können ist sehr nützlich für einen Soldaten."
—*Schlochow.*

The German Government devotes great attention to the training of the soldiers of the Empire in all kinds of athletic exercises, especially in the art of swimming. Government teachers of the art may be numbered by hundreds, and the general public are free to avail themselves of the advantages of the swimming schools and teachers so easy of access, which they do most generally. Hence the Germans may be said to be a nation of swimmers, and her soldiers would probably excel any in the world in swimming. The system taught is purely scientific, beginning with the swimming girdle with rope, this is adopted until the learner has acquired confidence, then diving begins, the legs being kept straight and close together, and so on, step by step, as in our own schools, only with more military precision. To show the excellence of German swimmers, I may mention that in Sept., 1879, at Bath, Long Island, in the contest for the American championship, a young German named Ernest Von Schoening, formerly a lieutenant in a Prussian regiment, who served on the staff of Prince Frederic Charles during the Franco-German War, 1870-71, won the belt, the ill-fated Captain Webb coming in second. An account of a grand aquatic fête (written by a correspondent of the *Jersey and Guernsey News*) which was held on the River Spree, near Berlin, cannot fail to be interesting. It is given *verbatim:*

"Last week we witnessed a spectacle of which there is scarcely an example in modern times, a 'Swimming Masquerade.' This grand spectacle was given by the pupils of the Royal Swimming School, of Berlin, in honor of its twenty-fifth anniversary, which has turned out in that time 23,365 good swimmers. At five o'clock p.m. 1,200 good swimmers, for the most part military men, met in the Barrack Square of the Infantry of the Guard, and proceeded to a row of white tents erected on the banks of the Spree, where they put on their costumes. At eight o'clock the following procession was seen to swim forward and pass before the admiring gaze of more than 40,000 spectators. First came a large flat boat, metamorphosed into a large arbor, beautifully decorated, in which were three bands, who executed *morceaux* of military music; then a car in the shape of a shell, in which was seated old Father Neptune, the god of the sea, with his hair and beard of reeds, and armed with a trident. This beautiful car was drawn by six dolphins, and surrounded by a band of Nereids and Tritons, the latter with trumpets and clashing cymbals. A large number of Indian musicians followed after, bearing on their heads brilliant plumes of variegated colors, and wearing collars and bracelets of coral and carrying Indian clubs. Then followed Scotchmen in Highland costume, Norwegians, Frenchmen, Spaniards, Italians, Russians and Portuguese, in their national costumes, in the order enumerated; next came Bacchus, the god of wine, seated upon a gigantic cask, crowned with vine leaves and ivy, brandishing in the air his thyrsus, with which he directed the grotesque evolutions of a hundred Bacchantes, who sported around his throne, following which came the king of frogs, seated on a car of reeds. A gigantic frog represented his majesty, and he was followed by a train of the same species, though less in bulk; and last, though not least, came 200 jolly Jack Tars, dressed in full man-of-war costume of various nationalities, and singing their own national songs. The immense crowds of people who were drawn together to witness this magnificent, though strange, sight, moved about on the banks of the river in carriages, on horseback, or on foot, some sailed about in small boats tastefully adorned with garlands and flowers."

An Anecdote of "Our Fritz."

That fine soldier, the late lamented Emperor Frederick III., the devoted husband of our beloved Queen's eldest daughter, the Princess Royal of England, was one of the strongest and most expert swimmers in the army, and during the summer months he was accustomed to take exercise early every morning in the vast garrison swimming school at Potsdam. He was a man of a jovial disposition, and by no means averse to a harmless practical joke, and he frequently amused himself, when the school has been full of huge guardsmen, by swimming rapidly up to some clumsy Anak, seizing him by the neck, and ducking his head under till he gasped enough; but the Emperor, or as he was best known as the Crown Prince, could take as well as play a joke, and one morning after ducking several of the famous first regiment of Grenadiers, in which he himself had graduated, he called out aloud, "Now you may try it on me if you can." He had hardly spoken the words when his neck was grasped from behind as by a vice, and he found himself compelled to perform several involuntary dives so prolonged that he presently fell short of breath and swallowed a considerable quantity of water, and soon cried out that he had more than enough, on which he was set free.

The Crown Prince turned to the grenadier and asked him his name, and in two days the Prince granted him a fortnight's furlough to visit his friends, at the same time generously forwarding the soldier money to defray his expenses. As my readers are aware, the Crown Prince became Emperor, but his life was cut short by a painful disease in his throat, his occupation of the Imperial throne being but a few months, and during the entire time and for a long period before, he was a confirmed invalid; but as he had throughout his life, when in ordinary health, displayed in the highest degree all the noblest qualities ever possessed by man, he exhibited the same heroic patience to the end— his most anxious thoughts seemed to be to spare others. Although a splendid specimen of a great general, he had an awful horror of war; and it is well known, had it been the will of God to spare him, his life as Emperor of Germany would have been devoted to the emancipation of his people from that constant feverish preparedness for war which must deprive the country of much of its natural wealth, besides being detrimental to its general internal advancement as a nation—so singularly remarkable for intelligence and great industry and patriotism.

It may or may not be known at some future date how important a part his truly devoted wife may have taken to bring about this well-known policy of the late Emperor, but there is one thing fully established, that the eldest daughter of our beloved Queen, the Princess Royal of England, was lovely and amiable in her youth, highly accomplished and devoted to duty as wife and mother, and in her exalted station showed herself never more happily employed than when ministering to those afflicted or distressed down to the humblest of the poor, and her future life, it is said, will be chiefly spent in this noble manner. The devotion and affection existing between herself and the Emperor was something sublime and heavenly; and all the English-speaking race throughout the globe, as well as the Germans and French, mourn with her in her comparatively early widowhood.

CHAPTER XXXVI.

ORNAMENTAL SWIMMING.

Good swimmers will in many ways
In water calm and still,
Find fresh chances for displays
Of their aquatic skill.

The writer believes that the instructions already imparted will be found sufficient for all purposes of general utility, and that practice alone is necessary to make perfect—he believes that some details of dexterity in the water, which come under the title of Ornamental Swimming, will be useful—although it is intended to be as concise as possible, owing to their accomplishment not being necessary in the ordinary sense of useful swimming, and also because good swimmers can find but little difficulty in their performance.

The illustrations accompanying each chapter, all of which have been drawn from life, will be a material help to the learner in mastering more readily the detailed instructions.

The above remarks are for the benefit of those who have systematically followed instructions from the commencement of the work.

To Swim Without Using Either Hand.

There are three modes of doing this.

1. *On the breast, with both hands in front.*—The body has to be held more erect than when one hand is used, the chest well forward, and the head thrown back. The further the hands are held forward the more closely the posture of the body has to approximate to a

Fig. 33.

perpendicular position, or that of treading water. The thumbs should be locked together, and the action of the limbs similar to that in the breast stroke (see Fig. 33).

2. *On the breast, with both hands behind the back.*—This mode is called the "butterfly," owing to a fancied resemblance the movements of the hands have to the wings of that insect, the hands flapping the

Fig. 34.

water at the small of the back. This is a more elegant, but a less useful way than either the preceding or following way (see Fig. 34.)

3. *With one hand before and the other hand behind the body.*—This is easily managed when swimming on the side. It is a useful plan when speed is required, as a rate equal to ordinary breast swimming

may be obtained by it. The action of the legs is similar to that used in the side stroke, but the body has to be kept more erect.

To Swim on the Back, Feet First, Without Using the Feet.

There are several methods.

1. The arms should be held straight and close to the side, while the hands, by a semi-circular turn of the wrist, scull the body.

2. Each arm to describe a quarter circle, the palms of the hands striking downward and backward like a paddle-wheel of a steamer.

3. The arms may be raised clean out of the water in making the negative stroke, and drawn through the water towards the head in the positive stroke, this method secures good speed when well executed.

4. The arms to be extended beyond the head, sculling the body along by the exterior and lateral movements of the wrist, similar to the feathering of an oar, this is both a simple and graceful method, although but little practised (see Fig. 35).

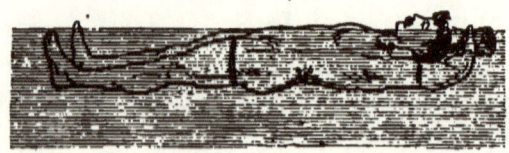

Fig. 35.

To Swim on the Back, Head First, Without Using the Feet.

The hands have simply to imitate the action of a duck's foot, being held down close to the thighs. The speed obtainable is very good, and the motion easy and natural.

To Swim Backwards on the Breast.

The swimmer is to place himself in the first position of the "breast stroke," that is, the legs and arms are to be extended in a line with the body, and kept close together. The legs must be held perfectly rigid, the action of the feet (a gentle motion up and down) is to proceed merely from the ankles, either upon the surface or immediately below it. The hands are to be drawn back with the palms together under the chin, and then the arms are to be straightened out in front, the water being pushed back with the palms of the hands; another method of using the hands is to keep the arms close together, and sculling as it were in small arcs with the hands.

Semi-Somersaults.

Semi-somersaults can be turned when swimming either on the breast or on the back.

ON THE BREAST.—To turn a somersault while swimming on the breast, two or three vigorous strokes are to be made, then the arms should be suddenly struck down, while the chin is pressed upon the chest, and the legs are doubled back upon the thighs, which have to be kept in a line with the body, these combined movements will at once throw the swimmer over on his back.

ON THE BACK.—This is done by using both arms and legs, the negative arm stroke should be made in the air, and the positive stroke, with considerable force, is to be made deep in the water, the

FIG. 36.

head being bent completely back and at the same time the knees are to be drawn up to the chest (see Fig. 36), these movements will cause the feet to travel faster than the body, and immediately half a revolution is performed. Although, to the uninitiated, they may appear difficult, a little confidence and practice is all that is required to make the movement a success.

Somersaults.

In order to turn a complete somersault, the swimmer who has mastered the semi-somersaults will find that he has only to make either the first or second series of movements a little more vigorously to complete the entire revolution, in either backward or forward somersaults. After the first revolution the body acquires a momentum, so that very little exertion is required to keep it revolving when once set in motion. The writer has known as many as fifteen complete revolutions made in rapid succession, and at one breath.

As in every other movement, the skill required can only come by constant practice. It will be well not to attempt too much at first, but gradually to master it, as the exercise is a rather exhausting one.

Leap-Frog.

Leap-frog can be played in the water as well as on land. Any number can play it, but four or six are plenty to make a good game.

They are to form into line three or four yards apart, "treading" water.

The hindmost one begins the sport, by swimming up to the one immediately in front of him, placing his hands upon the other's shoulders, forcing him down and himself up, and then springing over his head.

FIG. 37.

Having thus cleared the one, he proceeds with the others in the same manner, taking them in rotation till he arrives in front, where he "treads" water until all the others have gone over him in a similar way (see Fig. 37).

Some place their feet upon the shoulders of the undermost one, and then spring off; others, again, who are more expert, turn a front somersault while going over.

With good swimmers, this becomes a most exciting and amusing game.

The Steamer.

This feat is accomplished in the following manner: While lying on the back, start paddling with the hands close to the sides, at the same time rapidly beat the water by alternate blows of the feet, taking care to keep them well pointed.

If this is properly done, the swimmer drives up a shower of spray like that from the paddle-wheels of a steam-boat (see Fig. 38). The speed to be attained is considerable, and as the surface of the water is much agitated by the action of the legs, the swimmer appears to the uninitiated to move through the water with much greater speed than he really does.

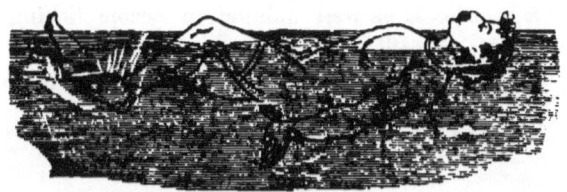

Fig. 38.

The writer has known several swimmers who could race for a short distance in this manner, and beat one who swam in the ordinary way.

The Propeller.

Turn over on the breast and strike out with the arms, as in the breast-stroke, raising the legs out of the water in rapid succession, and bringing them down smartly (see Fig. 39). The speed to be

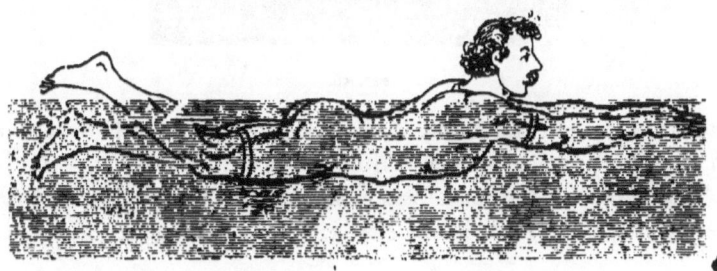

Fig. 39.

obtained in this method is much greater than in performing the "steamer," and much less fatiguing on the limbs. The motion of the feet resembles the action of the screw of a propeller, while the sound is precisely the same.

The writer once witnessed a race in which both contestants swam all the way from start to finish in this style.

The Pendulum.

Assume the position shown in perpendicular floating, throwing the head well back; then paddle with the hands, pressing the hands backward and downward; this will bring the toes up till they appear above the surface, in front of the body. By reversing the movement the heels will appear above the surface, behind the body, thus giving it the motion of the pendulum of a clock.

The Spinning Top.

The lungs require to be well inflated in accomplishing this feat, the posture to be assumed is that of swimming on the back with both feet out of the water. The hands on each side of the body press the

FIG. 40.

water in the same direction, that is, one hand presses it toward the body, while the other presses it from the body.

This imparts a horizontal rotary motion to the body, which within a certain limit increases in velocity with its duration (see Fig. 40).

The Washing-Tub.

The swimmer who makes the "washing-tub" does so in the following manner:

While lying on the back, he gathers his knees as near his chin as possible, and being thus packed into a compact form, he rotates rapidly by the action of the hands (see Fig. 41).

The secret of this feat is simply to work the hands with a downward pressure.

Fig. 41.

If this precaution is not taken, the "washing-tub" is sure to sink in the course of its first gyration.

Wrestling in the Water.

To wrestle in deep water requires considerable skill and activity. It is a first-rate method of determining which of two swimmers has

Fig. 42.

the most command over the element in which he is exerting his strength.

The rivals should "tread" water face to face, about two feet apart, at a given signal the right hand of each is placed upon his opponent's head. Then each of the combatants endeavours to force the other under water by pressure only. The one who first disappears beneath the surface is "vanquished" (see Fig 42).

Boxing in the Water.

To box in the water requires more skill than to wrestle, for in boxing both hands must be raised above the surface, while in wrestling only one is used in the contest, the other assisting the legs to support the body. The experts face one another a little less than arm's length apart, and give and receive blows in the usual manner,

Fig. 43.

treading water at the same time (see Fig 43). When properly executed it is good exercise, and at all times proves an interesting item in the programme of any first-class swimming tournament.

Another and simpler method is for the opponents to put on a cap, and let each then endeavor to knock his opponent's cap off. This affords capital amusement, besides giving the combatants full scope

SWIMMING AND LIFE-SAVING.

to determine which is the most skilful in the water, as well as increase their confidence in their own efforts, which they could not otherwise acquire.

The Revolving Feat.

The usual method adopted by every swimmer who wishes to accomplish this very difficult feat successfully, is to first float on the back with the arms by the side, the palm of one turned downward close to the surface, the other hand deeper with the palm turned up; then, by jerking the body, pressing the water down with the palm of one hand and up with the palm of the other, the swimmer is turned over on his face. By repeating the action of the hands at suitable

FIG. 44.

intervals, the body is kept rolling (see Fig. 44). Very few swimmers can achieve this, unless in a stream current or lying broadside on the waves of the sea where the motion of the water greatly facilitates that of the body. Still fewer can continue it more than a few seconds, the difficulty being to take a breath while revolving. The most elegant manner of performing this feat is with the hands clasped beyond the head, with legs and arms straight and rigid, when the cause of revolution is imperceptible to the spectator. The motion, though tardy at first, is accelerative, so if continued for a time, the velocity becomes considerable. This manœuvre is, by many considered the "masterpiece" of swimming. The writer only knows of five persons who could accomplish this clever aquatic feat in "still" water.

To Swim Holding One Foot.

There are four methods of doing this:
1st. The right foot being held in the left hand.
2nd. The left foot being held in the right hand.

3rd. The left foot being held in the left hand.

4th. The right foot being held in the right hand.

In the first and second methods the swimmer has to lie on his breast, the disengaged hand and foot having to be worked as in the dog stroke.

In the third and fourth methods the swimmer is to lie on his side, performing the same stroke rather more obliquely.

To Swim Holding the Feet in One or Both Hands.

To execute this feat the swimmer has to turn on his back, to draw the feet up, both big toes touching, to open his knees, to keep the chest well up and expanded, to throw the head well back, to hold both big toes in either of his hands, and to steady the body, face upwards, with the unused hand. If the arms be crossed at the wrists, one foot may be held in each hand. This feat can only be accomplished by an adept, as the body has to be carefully balanced. A very slight departure from the balance position will cause the body to roll over face downward. This must be carefully avoided.

Hurdle Races.

Swimming races may be varied by the introduction of special features, such as hurdle racing, duck hunt, water polo, etc.

The hurdles should be made of rope, at least twenty-five feet long, the end attached to large floats which would bring them about two feet above the surface of the water. Any number of these may be used, according to the instructions of the committee of management. The breast stroke should be used, the swimmer pressing his hands forcibly downwards, which will enable him to spring up and grasp the hurdle, over which he jumps as in "leap frog." When a number of contestants take part in this amusement, it furnishes considerable sport to the spectators, besides exhibiting the activity of the swimmers. Edward Corlett, of the Dolphin Swimming Club, has won two silver medals for proficiency in this style of racing.

Egg Hunt.

Place two or three dozen of eggs in a wire basket and lower them into ten or twelve feet of water, then let a number of expert divers bring up as many as they can unbroken, diving one after another. The one bringing up the most at one dive to be considered the winner.

Duck Hunt.

This amusement will be found of great utility in testing the capabilities of the swimmer to remain under water for any considerable length of time. A number of good swimmers, say fifteen, take part in the sport; one of them acts as the duck; he has a few minutes' start; the others then plunge in and endeavor to reach him; when they approach too close the duck dives, and swimming under water as long as he can contain his breath, re-appears in an entirely different direction, keeping this up until he is exhausted, when another swimmer takes his place, and so the sport continues.

Tub Race.

This proves a very amusing event in the sports of a swimming club. Each contestant provides his own tub and paddles. The start should be made direct from the wharf, or landing stage, with each person seated in their tub, the paddle in the right hand, the left hand on the wharf, with an intervening space of at least five feet, to prevent any collision at the start.

FIG. 45.

The course should be out, say 500 yards, around the buoy, turning from right to left, and home again. All contestants must turn the buoy in that way, thus insuring an interesting race, and fair play for all who take part in the sport.

Water Polo.

In this sport ten or more persons are provided with casks, in imitation of horses, and bats with blades at both ends, similar to a canoe paddle, which serve the double purpose of maintaining their equilibrium and propelling them in any direction, as shown in the illustration on next page.

The goals should be made of floats, surmounted by a flag, two at each end of the course—say ten feet apart, abreast of one another,—through which the ball must pass. The flags should be of different colors to designate the sides, the men wearing badges of similar colors for the same object.

Fig. 46.

The ball should be a hollow rubber one, which will be found sufficiently buoyant for the purpose; the men use their paddles in the same manner as a bat or shinny, endeavoring to force the ball between the flags, as in our own national game of lacrosse.

CHAPTER XXXVII.

LEARNING TO SWIM WITH THE AID OF A TEACHER.

Parents can assist materially in teaching their children to swim. Illustration on page 79 will show how this can best be accomplished with the aid of a pole, rope and belt—the latter should be from six to eight inches broad—of cotton webbing, or some other strong

Learning to Swim with the Aid of a Teacher.

material. Should the lesson be given off a wharf or pier, the pupil should enter the water at the shallow end, wading out till breast high, then the person standing on the pier should hand the bather the belt to be put on, or it can be adjusted before entering the water. The teacher, by raising the pole, will bring the learner to a horizontal position in the water.

Then proceed, according to the instructions given under the head of "Breast stroke." Do not "duck" or otherwise frighten the learner. Many pupils have a natural timidity of water; such persons require to be gently treated and encouraged, so as to get rid of their fears.

CHAPTER XXXVIII.

PUBLIC SWIMMING SCHOOLS.

The citizens of Canada should make every effort posssible to extend a knowledge of the art of swimming by erecting as many buildings of this kind as possible, in order that Canadians may some day excel the world in swimming, as they now do in rowing. It is to be regretted that, while bathing is so generally recommended by the highest medical authorities, it should be so seldom practised.

Professor Blaikie said, when speaking of the propriety of establishing public swimming baths, "he had often, while studying the classics, been astonished that in devoting so much attention to their languages, they practised so few of the customs of the ancients. Gymnastics were absolutely necessary to the preservation of health, and bathing formed one very important part of gymnastics. . . . Those gymnastics which excite, and those that soothe the physical frame, were as necessary to the development and perfect toning of the properties of the body, as education was to those of the mind." In many of the public swimming baths in England, where class distinction is much more marked than it is in Canada, where the spirit of a pure democracy prevails, there are three distinct grades of baths, styled first, second and third class, the scale of charges being graduated according to the accommodation. For instance, the Marylebone Baths, of London, England, contains not only the gem bath of seventy-three feet long for gentlemen, and one of forty-five feet long for ladies, but a second-class bath of tepid water, sixty six feet long, the charge for admittance being threepence; also a third-class bath of similar dimensions, for which twopence only is charged. All of these are admirably lighted, airy and clean—even the third-class bath being lined with white brick. Public baths should always have an ample supply of bathing drawers, etc., so as to be an inducement to visitors to take a plunge; the luxury, when once enjoyed, will then be desired. Every swimming club is, or ought to be, provided with a proper uniform. The uniform of the Dolphin Swimming Club consists of a blue serge combination suit (one piece), of the regulation pattern, from neck to knee. The suit is neatly trimmed with red and white, the whole constituting the tri-color. Across the breast are the letters D. S. C., forming a handsome and attractive uniform. When aquatic entertainments are given, and ladies come to witness them, "regulation dress" is very properly insisted on, and some sort of costume should at all times be compulsory.

Public baths are a blessing to every locality in which they are situated; if it were not for them, many thousands in large cities would be doomed to live out their lot on earth in pent-up, ill-ventilated dwellings, where fresh air and the genial sun enter not; their journey to their place of daily toil is by roads alternately muddy and dusty, and they would never, but for those public baths, enjoy the blessing of a thorough ablution, thus relieving the monotony of their lives, and giving poor, abused and tired nature a chance.

Encouragement of Swimming at Public Schools.

With the view of stimulating our Canadian youth to greater exertion in the preservation of life from drowning, I thought it advisable to present a representation of the handsome silver medallion awarded by the Royal Humane Society for "Swimming Exercises,

with reference to Saving Life from Drowning;" the motto on the obverse side of the medal, "Nare Est Alienam Nosse Salutem," the free translation of which is, "The ability to swim makes one know how to save others," will commend itself to everybody, while the engraving is sufficiently explicit in itself for the most obtuse intellect; since the first award of these medals, swimming in clothes has received a decided impetus. The following anecdote, taken from the Royal Humane Society's Report of 1885, will prove interesting showing, as it does, the great value of these exercises in training our youth for gallant deeds :

"The swimming competitions under the Society's rules, with reference to saving life from drowning, have now been carried on for four years, and judging by the general opinion expressed by headmasters of schools and training ships, they appear to be not only popular, but instructive to the swimmer in the important matter of saving drowning persons.

"Apropos of this, and as an inducement to other school-boys to follow a good example, it is worth mentioning that a Tunbridge school pupil, named Leonard Lockhart Miller, aged fifteen, on the 22nd of October last, gallantly plunged into the Medway and rescued another lad, of eleven years of age, from drowning. It appears that the younger boy, after becoming immersed, was carried out to the centre of the river by the strong current, and sank three times, when Miller swam out with all his clothes on and, after diving, succeeded in bringing the boy to the surface.

"It is stated that the salvor had gained his experience in saving life by competing, at his school, for the Royal Humane Society's swimming prize. .

."Miller has been awarded the bronze medal for this act."

CHAPTER XXXIX.

PUBLIC SWIMMING BATHS.

The Wiman Island Swimming Baths.

The author takes this opportunity of referring to the above Strange though it may seem that in a go-a-head city like Toronto, with so vast a population and so much wealth, with her beautiful bay and magnificent lake at her feet, yet until the year 1882 there were no public baths erected. In that year Erastus Wiman, Esq., a former citizen, but long since residing elsewhere, removed this blot from our civic history by erecting the beautiful pavilion, known as above, entirely at his own expense. The ground was leased at a nominal rent, and, when everything was complete, Mr. Wiman conveyed the whole by trustees as a gift to the city of Toronto, with the condition that the profits should be expended on beautifying and improving the property and its surroundings. The building is most admirably situated, having the Toronto Bay on one side and the open waters of Lake Ontario on the other, thus affording abundant bathing facilities. The accommodation for ladies and gentlemen is complete, and altogether the place is most enjoyable for visitors, whether bathers or non-bathers; and every season the numbers who go there testify to its popularity.

There is one point of great importance that the management of places of this kind should ever carefully see to, and that is, every possible precaution should be taken to prevent accidents, and, in the event of danger, the resources to effect rescue from drowning should be, humanly speaking, perfect. The original trustees are: John J. Withrow, President; James B. Boustead, R. W. Elliott, W. B. McMurrich, and William Gooderham, Esq.; Mr. Jas. B. Marshall is the present manager.

Extract from the Toronto *Evening News*, Oct. 12th, 1885: "In July, 1882, Captain Andrews was appointed instructor of swimming by the Wiman Bath Trust, which position he has occupied ever since. The Captain's class-book contains the autographs of 189 ladies and 99 gentlemen, whom he has taught this useful accomplishment. Captain Andrews' efforts have been rewarded by many testimonials from his pupils at the close of each season, among which is a handsome watch-chain presented by some of his scholars this year."

In addition to the above, he received a testimonial from John J. Withrow, President of the Wiman Bath Trust, acknowledging his valuable services as a swimmer and life-saver.

The West End Island Baths.

Following the example set by Mr. Wiman in 1882, a number of citizens, forming a limited company, erected a comfortable and commodious building on the west end of the Island, near Hanlan's Point, for the special accommodation of the citizens residing in the West End. A substantial bridge was also erected connecting the baths with Han-

Association Hall, Toronto.

lan's Point. Bathers have the full enjoyment of the open waters of the lake, and receive all necessary attention and comforts for a small charge. The baths are well patronized.

The Y. M. C. A. Baths, Toronto.

These baths are on the basement floor of the building at Yonge Street, corner of McGill, and, in common with every other branch of the physical department, offer every inducement for the comfort of bathers. Indeed, it may truly be said, that the directors have left nothing to be desired, everything in the department being well and skilfully planned, and the materials and workmanship are the best that money could purchase, and the excellence of the arrangements are fully appreciated by the members; the fact that over 200 persons enjoy the different branches of the exercises sufficiently prove their popularity.

There is a swimming-bath 50 ft. x 16 ft., with a depth on entry of 4 ft. 6 inches, increasing to 5 ft. 6 in., containing 25,000 gallons of water, which is changeable at pleasure, and is maintained at a temperature of about 70 degrees during the winter months. There are separate bath-rooms of the ordinary kind, with hot and cold water, also shower and needle baths, with hot and cold water supply, which the bather can regulate as desired. Access to all the privileges of this splendid establishment, including library and reading room, may be had for $7.00 per annum. The advantages of membership can hardly be over-estimated, and an inspection of the concern will amply repay visitors. The courteous and efficient General Secretary, Mr. Wm. McCulloch, is noted for his kind attention to all, especially to strangers, who are sure to receive at his hands a cordial welcome.

CHAPTER XL.

SWIMMING RACES.

To attain success in a swimming competition, the horizontal position is preferable to all others, as it enables the swimmer to get over more ground, or rather water, at a much greater speed than can be obtained by any other method.

Fish adopt the horizontal position naturally, as it offers the least resistance to their movements, and the nearer men come to that position in swimming the better chance they have of success. Marine architects are beginning to realize this fact, and our modern vessels are constructed with a view to so equalizing the vessel's tonnage over its entire surface as to decrease the draught, and consequently increase the speed. Canada, whose navy ranks fifth among the maritime powers, has many "Greyhounds of the sea" built upon this principle, such as the steamer *Cibola* and others, equal to any in the world for speed and safety. A great many self-taught swimmers endeavor to swim with the body too deep in the water, the primary cause of this is the fact that they draw their legs up underneath the body instead of laterally, as already described in the breast stroke. The frog, so frequently quoted as a model for swimmers, draws his legs up laterally instead of under the body, thus obtaining a much more powerful stroke, its forepaws are tucked under the chin, and are used simply to buoy the body up near the surface, while all the propelling power is centred in its legs. Catch one and place it in a tub of water and see for yourself. The nearer you can bring your own legs to kick like the frog the better, adding to this knowledge the information given in the chapter on the breast stroke.

If there is a tendency to get out of this correct position of the body by depression, the chest should be laid with more force upon the water, and the head a little thrown back, thus raising the chin and clearing the waves, at the same time the limbs should be raised (but not above the surface), this effort will replace the body in the true horizontal position. Care must be taken not to make the strokes *too* near the surface, which would cause foaming and splashing. The strokes should be made so as to obtain a good grip of the water, and this is obtained not by increasing the angle of inclination of the whole body, but by depressing it uniformly through its entire length. It is quite easy to understand the theory that the lighter the draught, the greater the speed, as described above in relation to vessels. A few words regarding respiration will doubtless prove valuable. When the arms are extended and the legs drawn up ready for the propelling stroke, a deep breath should be inhaled. When making the stroke, it should be expelled. You will find this very useful, in a swimming contest especially, as it prevents you becoming exhausted or out of breath, and will enable you to remain fresh and buoyant for a very long time, besides adding greatly to the force of your strokes.

CHAPTER XLI.

SWIMMING CLUBS.

The Amateur Swimming Association of Great Britain.

This association was established for the purpose of incorporating the various swimming clubs throughout the Empire under one federal government, its membership comprising all the leading clubs of Great Britain and Ireland, while its rules and regulations commend themselves to all swimming clubs throughout the world.

The accompanying illustration shows the handsome medal awarded by the association for proficiency in the art. This medal is greatly prized by those who are fortunate enough to obtain one.

The Liverpool Swimming Club.

This club is one of the largest in England, with a membership of over six hundred persons.

The magnificent prizes awarded at the annual competitions are, for the most part, very valuable and attractive; consisting of twenty guinea silver cups and other silver articles of utility and ornament, in addition to the usual number of medals. Through the generosity of the citizens, as well as the extent of its membership, the club are enabled to offer a large assortment of costly prizes for competition year after year. The Dolphin Swimming Club would be delighted if the citizens of Toronto would enable them to do likewise.

The Ilex Swimming Club.

This club meets in the celebrated Marylebone Baths, London, and is one of the leading clubs of the great metropolis, with a membership of several hundred. Its annual competitions have developed a number of first-class swimmers.

The Montreal Swimming Club.

This is the largest swimming club in the Dominion, and was organized by Lieut.-Colonel Labranche in August, 1876, having now a membership of over twelve hundred persons, including many of the leading citizens of Montreal, who cheerfully support by contributions the maintenance of the club in the highest state of efficiency. The club baths are situated on St. Helen's Island, and are both commodious and comfortable. The grounds surrounding the baths are beautifully laid out. Visitors to these baths receive all due attention and kindness. Admission is by ticket; each member having the right to introduce visitors to the city of Montreal, and on this introduction each visitor can enjoy the use of the baths, etc., for fourteen days. A swimming master is always in attendance to instruct novices, boats are provided in case of accident, and the club ferry is at hand for the convenience of visitors crossing and recrossing the river.

The Dolphin Swimming Club, Toronto.

This popular swimming club was organized in 1881 by Captain W. D. Andrews, R.H.S., for the purpose of extending the knowledge of swimming with the view to the greater preservation of life from drowning. Every member is carefully instructed in the proper methods for restoring the apparently drowned. He is also shown the best means to adopt in rescuing drowning persons by swimming to their relief.

The annual swimming tournament is held at the Wiman Island Baths each season, at which numerous and valuable prizes are awarded to the winners.

Since its organization the club has awarded nine gold medals of the first class, two handsome silver cups, and forty-five silver medals, besides numerous other valuable prizes for skill and dexterity in the art of swimming.

It is the intention of the club to offer special prizes for competition by the pupils attending the Public Schools. This, it is hoped, will secure a large share of support from the citizens generally.

DOLPHIN SWIMMING CLUB.

OFFICERS 1889.

Honorary President:

ERASTUS WIMAN, ESQ., - - - - *Founder of the Wiman Baths.*

Honorary Vice-Presidents:

JOHN J. WITHROW, ESQ.   JAS. B. BOUSTEAD, ESQ.
EDWARD J. TACKLEY,   THOS. J. DARLING, ESQ.,
    Hon. Sec. Amateur Swimming Association.   *Hon. Sec. Montreal Swimming Club.*

WILLIAM GOODERHAM, ESQ.   ROBERT ELLIOTT, ESQ.
H. P. GOOD, ESQ.   A. F. PIRIE, ESQ.

President, - - - - CAPTAIN W. D. ANDREWS,
    Honorary Medal and Clasps, Royal Humane Society.

Vice-Presidents, - - - ARTHUR PRICE, ALFRED POTTER.
Umpire, - - - - CAPTAIN C. G. HARSTON,
    Honorary Medal, Royal Humane Society.

Secretary, - - - - C. T. PRICE.
Treasurer, - - - - R. E. MOSEY.
Captain, - - - - J. L. RAWBONE.
    Honorary Medal, Royal Humane Society.

Club Stewards, - - - E. A. WILLIAMS, G. T. GOLDSTONE.

AUDACES FORTUNA JUVAT.

LIST OF MEDALLISTS SINCE 1881

ROLL OF HONOR. LIFE-SAVING MEDALLISTS.

" Rescue the Perishing."

Captain W. D. ANDREWS, L.S.S., Five Gold Life-Saving Medals of the first class, with additional clasps; Bronze Medal of the Royal Humane Society, with clasps, etc. Capt. WM. WARD, Silver Medal and clasp, R.H.S. J. D. PATRY, Bronze Medal, R.H.S. Capt. J. L. RAWBONE, D.S.C., Wiman Gold Medal; Bronze Medal, Royal Humane Society. Sergt. A. E. PRICE, R.G., Silver Medal, D.S.C. HUGH V. PAYNE, Silver Medal, R.H S. Capt. C. G. HARSTON, R.G., Bronze Medal, Royal Humane Society. THOMAS ROBINSON, Silver Medal, W.H.S. FRANK TINNING, Bronze Medal, R.H.S.

Honorary Medallists:

C. T. PRICE, Andrews' Silver Medal.   R. E. MOSEY, Andrews' Silver Medal.

Silver Cup Winners:

W. H. DURAND, Silver Cup, 1883.   G. W. HYSLOP, Silver Cup, 1885.

Lady Prize Winners:

Miss ADA PHILLIPS.   Miss MABEL PLATTS.

Swimming Medallists:

" May the Best Men Win."

Capt. W. D. ANDREWS, one gold medal. A. DIXON, two silver medals.
Sergt. A. E. PRICE, five silver medals. ALFRED POTTER, five silver medals.
CHARLES PRICE, two silver medals. ALBERT BROWN, two silver medals.
CHARLES POWELL, one silver medal. FRANK PRICE, two silver medals.
HERBERT COWAN, one silver medal. GEORGE PLUMB, one silver medal.
CHARLES NURSE, one silver medal. G. F. WEBBER, one silver medal.
J. L. RAWBONE, one gold, one silver medal. J. D. PATRY, four silver medals.
J. SCHMIDT, three silver medals.
G. T. GOLDSTONE, one silver medal. ERNEST PRICE, two silver medals.
J. M. LANDFIELD, two silver medals. W. SMITH, one silver medal.
F. W. MATTHEWS, one silver medal. M. F. SMITH, three silver medals.
D. MOSSMAN, one silver medal. F. HAWKINS, two silver medals.
C. DIXON, one silver medal. E. CORLETT, one gold, one silver medal.

Dolphin Swimming Club.

Rules.

1. That this club be called the "Dolphin Swimming Club," and that its purpose be the encouragement and teaching of swimming, and saving of life from drowning; and that the crest and motto, "Honor, Heroism, Humanity," designed for the club by Captain Andrews, be adopted, and the same become the emblem of the club; and that the club colors be red, white, and blue.

2. That the membership of this club be open to all, but only amateurs shall be permitted to compete in the sports of the club during the year, except in an open race, which may include professionals. The following is the correct definition of an amateur:

An amateur is one who has never competed for a money prize, declared wager, or staked bet; who has never taught, pursued, or assisted in the practice of swimming or any other athletic exercise as a means of pecuniary gain; and who has not, knowingly or without protest, taken part in any competition or exhibition with any one who is not an amateur.

3. That all members appear in the regulation costume of the club, both at practices and competitions.

4. That the club costume consist of a combination suit of shirt and drawers, in one piece. Material of blue serge, with red and white trimmings—the whole forming a tri-color; the club to furnish the letters D. S. C., in white, to be worn on the breast of the uniform.

5. That the annual subscription be two dollars for all persons over eighteen years of age, who will be known as *senior members*, and one dollar for all under that age, who will be styled *junior members*.

6. Only those members whose subscriptions are paid in full will be allowed to compete in the annual swimming tournament.

7. The annual swimming tournament will be held as early in the season as possible, when medals and other valuable prizes will be offered for competition.

8. That the committee of management have full control of all matters appertaining to the annual sports of the club, and all entries must be made with the Secretary, to whom, also, all entrance fees must be paid at least five days previous to the date fixed for the tournament.

9. That the gold medal of this club be awarded only for bravery in saving life from drowning, and that in cases where the winner of this medal again performs an act of heroism equal in merit to that

92   SWIMMING AND LIFE-SAVING.

which gained him the medal, a gold clasp may be added for each succeeding act.

10. That the silver medal be awarded to the winners of each event in the annual swimming races, and that such winners shall not further compete during the races of the year, so that the honors of the club may be fairly divided among its members

11. That the officers of this club consist of a President, Vice-President, Secretary and Treasurer, who shall be elected at the annual general meeting; these officers to be *ex-officio* members of the committee of management.

12. That the Captaincy of the club be given to the best long-distance swimmer among the members, the race for this office being free to all, the winner to enjoy his title so long as he maintains his supremacy.

13. All the business of the club to be controlled by the managing committee.

14. This committee to consist of nine members elected annually, five of whom shall form a quorum. The committee to meet bi-monthly during the season; these meetings are open to every *bona fide* member.

15. That the annual meeting be held immediately after the swimming tournament, when the prizes shall be presented, the officers for the ensuing year elected, and the committe appointed for the coming season.

CHAPTER XLII.

THE PROPER METHOD TO BE ADOPTED IN RESCUING DROWNING PERSONS BY SWIMMING TO THEIR RELIEF.

"Courage and humanity are the greatest of Nature's adornments."
—*Darling.*

This is something that every swimmer ought to know. Many of our best swimmers shrink involuntarily from making the attempt to save a fellow-creature in danger of perishing.

The first requisites in order to effect a rescue successfully are courage and presence of mind. Always approach the person in danger from behind. If clothed seize the person by the collar of his coat, or if naked by the hair of the head, press your knee in the small of his back, as shown in Fig. 47; this will straighten out the body horizontally, while the strain upon the arm of the rescuer in towing him will keep the face of the person rescued clear of the

Fig. 47.

water (Fig. 48), thus enabling him to breathe freely, the rescuer using his right arm and limbs to enable him to reach the shore or other position of safety.

Fig. 48.

When the person endangered keeps turning round, as some have done with the writer, it is best to swim around them until the person can be so seized as mentioned, from behind, thus avoiding the drowning person's grasp; which is very tenacious. Should you, however, happen to be seized by the grasp of a drowning person, which so frequently proves fatal to both, do not lose your presence of mind, but having taken a full breath allow yourself to sink with the person. In nine cases out of ten he will let go his hold and endeavor to reach the surface, believing that you are also in danger of drowning.

Should, however, the grasp be retained, endeavor to force them away by pressing the knees against the abdomen. In either case you can then seize the person from behind, rise to the surface and strike out for shore, as already described.

FIG. 49.

The writer has frequently encountered persons who acted in both ways, and is therefore speaking from a long experience.

Another good plan is for the rescuer to throw himself upon his back, placing the person's head on the pit of his own stomach, as shown in Fig. 49, kicking out vigorously with his legs at right angles,

FIG. 50.

as in back swimming, having previously taken a line of alignment to steer by.

In this way he can accomplish a rescue with much greater ease. The author on one occasion rescued two persons in this way, for which he received the Bronze Medal of the Royal Humane Society. When

Fig. 51.

the person has sunk and it becomes necessary to dive, you can be guided by the air bubbles which rise to the surface, perpendicularly if the water is still, and diagonally if the stream is running (Fig. 50). Immediately on reaching the bottom, seize the person, a slight jerk will suffice to raise the body, and the surface may be reached in a few seconds by pressing the water downward with the disengaged hand and both feet in the usual way (Fig. 51).

It may be, owing to the discoloration of the water or other causes, the person who sank reaches the surface while the would-be rescuer is searching beneath. In such a case it is best to await above for a re-appearance.

The following case is recorded, being interesting:

A man accidentally fell into a river; being unable to swim, he sank almost immediately; a brave young fellow, in the desire to save his life, dived in the direction he was last seen. While the rescuer was down searching for the man who sank, the latter rose to the surface. The rescuer coming up, found the man had sunk for the second time; instead of diving again the fellow swam round until the man again came to the surface, when the rescuer seized him by the back and towed him ashore.

Before making the attempt at rescue, divest yourself of as much clothing as possible, tearing them off if necessary, at all events remove your boots if time permits. There may be cases when time will not permit the removal of any portion of clothing. It was particularly so in the rescue of a young man in Toronto Bay, August, 1884, when the author plunged in with all his clothes on, including boots, but was seized by the drowning youth in such a manner that both sank; rising to the surface, however, he struck out again for the shore and reached shallow water in safety.

I have been frequently asked why a drowning person rises to the surface two or three times. My own belief is that the air remaining in the lungs may not become entirely exhausted at the first immersion, consequently the body possesses sufficient buoyancy to rise again. This may be repeated a second or even a third time, according to the quantity of air in the lungs.

The rescuer should at all times be governed by circumstances in his efforts to reach the shore, always taking care to avoid wasting his strength against an adverse tide, by which he may be lost as well as the person for whom he risked his life; whereas if he had patiently floated on his back, a boat or other aid may arrive, and his effort be thus crowned with success.

CHAPTER XLIII.

DIRECTIONS FOR RESTORING THE APPARENTLY DROWNED, RECOMMENDED BY THE DOLPHIN SWIMMING CLUB.

"While there's life there's hope."—*Old Proverb.*

Rule 1.—Proceed at once to employ means to restore breathing. Do not delay this in order to procure shelter, warmth, stimulants, etc.

Rule 2.—Remove all obstructions to breathing. Instantly loosen or cut apart all neck and waist bands; turn the patient on the face with the head lower than the feet; stand astride the hips with your face toward the head, and locking your fingers together under the

Fig. 52.

abdomen, raise the body as high as you can without lifting the forehead off the ground, and give the body a smart jerk to remove mucus and water from the mouth and wind-pipe. Hold the body suspended long enough to count one, two, three, four, five, repeating the jerk more gently two or three times (see Fig. 52).

Fig. 53.

Rule 3.—Next place the patient on the back on a flat surface inclined a little from the feet upwards, raise and support the head and shoulders on a firm cushion, or folded article of dress, placed under the shoulder blades, cleanse the mouth and nostrils, open the mouth, draw forward the patient's tongue, securing it there either by holding it with the fingers, or by a piece of string or elastic band placed over it and under the chin (see Fig. 53).

Rule 4.—Grasp the patient's arms just above the elbows, and draw the arms gently and steadily upwards until they meet above the head (this is for the purpose of drawing air into the lungs). Keep the arms in this position for two seconds, and then turn them down and press them gently and firmly against the sides of the chest, pressing at the same time on the breast and abdomen (this is with the object of pressing air out of the lungs) (see Fig. 54). Pressing on the abdomen by an assistant will aid expiratory efforts. Repeat these measures alternately and deliberately until a spontaneous effort to breathe is perceived, immediately upon which cease to imitate the movements of breathing, and proceed to induce circulation and warmth.

FIG. 54.

Rule 5.—To excite respiration, during the employment of the foregoing methods, excite the nostrils with snuff, or smelling salts, or tickle the throat with a feather. Rub the chest and face briskly, and dash cold and hot water alternately upon the patient.

Do not be soon discouraged. Remember that at any time within two hours your efforts may be successful.

Rule 6.—To induce circulation and warmth, after breathing is commenced, wrap the patient in warm blankets, and apply bottles of hot water, hot bricks, or anything to restore heat.

Warm the head nearly as fast as the body, lest convulsions should be induced. Rubbing the body with warm cloths, or with the hands, and slapping the fleshy parts, may assist to restore warmth and breathing.

If the patient can swallow with safety, give hot coffee, tea, milk, or spirits. Allow the patient to have abundance of fresh air.

Wharf owners, and other persons residing near the water, should keep a coil of rope and pieces of boards in some convenient place, ready for immediate use.

To Persons who Cannot Swim.

If you get into water beyond your depth, do not plunge, struggle, or throw your hands and arms out of the water. "Tread water" in the erect position by moving the feet up and down, at the same time paddling with the hands, keeping them under water. If any person approaches to rescue you, preserve your presence of mind and do *not* grasp him; do what he tells you. If any small object be thrown to you, place it under your chest or arm-pits, and do not struggle to raise yourself out of the water; your head will not go under if you follow these instructions, and you may keep your mouth and nose above water long enough for assistance to arrive.

By considering these directions carefully now, you will be less apt to lose your presence of mind, should occasion arise for acting on them.

Parents should have their children taught to swim. Many drowning accidents might thereby be averted.

Note to the reader.—Believing that a great many lives might annually be saved if a proper knowledge of the methods of restoring the apparently drowned were more widely circulated, Captain W. D. Andrews, R.H.S., suggested the advisability of the D. S. C. publishing a complete set of rules for the guidance of wharf owners, boatmen and others residing near the water. Acting upon that suggestion, we present you with the above rules, with the hope that you will preserve them, so that should occasion arise you may possibly be the means of saving one or more lives.

By order of the Committee.

C. T. PRICE, *Secretary*,

DOLPHIN SWIMMING CLUB.

N.B.—Please post up these directions in a conspicuous place.

"AMICUS HUMANI GENERIS."

CHAPTER XLIV.

THE ROYAL HUMANE SOCIETY.

INSTITUTED 1774.

PATRON—HER MAJESTY THE QUEEN.

"Drag the pale victim from the whelming wave,
And snatch the body from the floating grave;
Breathe in the lips re-animating fire
Till, warmed to second life, the drowned respire."

—*Pratt.*

For the benefit of my readers who may not be familiar with the history of this truly noble Society, I give the following brief sketch, which cannot fail to be interesting:

As the year of its institution denotes, the Society is now in existence 115 years. It is supported by voluntary contributions. It confers honorary rewards for saving life from drowning. It collects and circulates the most approved and effectual methods for recovering persons apparently drowned. It provides suitable apparatus in and around London for rescuing persons from drowning. It encourages swimming exercises at public schools, by awarding silver medallions and certificates. These are also open to the boys of H. M. training ships.

About the middle of the last century, the penetrating genius of Dr. I. Fothergill (distinguished already by his advanced knowledge of different branches of his noble profession) addressed a paper to the Royal Society, in which he maintained the possibility of saving many lives—of those apparently drowned—without risking anything; and, although this theory was new, at the time little interest seemed to have been aroused in the minds of the medical philosophers of his time. The glory of proving the correctness of the theory was reserved for a later period. This was first attempted by M. Reaumer, an ingenious foreigner, who had successfully resuscitated several persons who were apparently drowned, in Switzerland, in the year 1767, reporting the facts to the Academy of Sciences, at Paris.

The city of Amsterdam soon after instituted a society to promote efforts in the same direction. The memoirs of this society were translated into English in 1773 by Dr. Cogan, for the purpose of convincing the English people of the truth of Dr. Fothergill's theory;

and Dr. Cogan's work fell into the hands of Dr. Hawes, who zealously devoted his life to the cause he seems to have delighted in pursuing. That he met with great difficulty in establishing the theory is apparent; but Dr. Hawes nobly stuck to his work, even paying, out of his own pocket, rewards for cases to be brought to him of persons who had been rescued, but still apparently dead—and so several such persons were restored by him, and the rewards offered publicly were duly paid. The doctor's generosity evoked a strong sympathy, and Dr. Cogan came to his aid, and both these gentlemen, on consultation, seem to have concluded that it was desirable to establish the Humane Society—and they were supported by thirty-two friends—and with these Drs. Hawes and Cogan laid the foundation of the Society. Until the end of Dr. Hawes' life the institution continued to receive his unremitting attention and vigilant care. Of the thirty-two gentlemen who had the distinguished honor of establishing, in conjunction with Dr. Hawes and Dr. Cogan, the Royal Humane Society, it may be worth mentioning, six were medical men, six were clergymen, two Fellows of the Royal Society—the remainder are not designated as to their calling, but it may be assumed they were merchants, probably having interests connected with the shipping trade. The incorporation of the Society exhibits most impressively what power there is in a single mind when moved to accomplish objects of a benign character; and to the persevering efforts of Dr. Hawes the English nation is indebted for the formation of a Society, the benefits of which are enjoyed wherever a British ship sails. The Society's usefulness is extending more and more every year, as indeed it deserves to do; its honors are eagerly sought after, and its decorations are proudly worn by heroes on land and sea, and there is no doubt this will be the case for all time.

As to the work actually accomplished, it may be mentioned that up to 31 Dec., 1888, over 23,000 cases have received awards, consisting of gold, silver, and bronze medals, additional clasps, certificates of honor on parchment, vellum, etc., as well as pecuniary rewards.

There are over 274 life-saving apparatus stations supplied by the Society, with the following apparatus : The life-buoy; the rope-drag; the pole-drag; the bar-drag; the hand-line, for icemen; the cork-jacket, for icemen; the ice-ladder; ropes; ice-boats; ice-sleighs for carrying the ordinary boats on the ice.

The Society's principal Receiving-House is on the north bank of the Serpentine River, Hyde-Park, built by the Society on ground granted by His late Majesty, King George the Third, and subsequently extended by His late Majesty King William the Fourth, in 1834. Proper attendants and warm baths are in constant readiness during the bathing and skating seasons, to prevent the fatal or injurious effects of any accident. Boats with proper boatmen, supplied with drags, etc., are always in attendance during the bathing season on the Serpentine, to render immediate assistance in event of any accident occurring.

In 1888, the awards of the Society are as follows : one gold medal (Stanhope); 25 silver medals; 172 bronze medals; 8 clasps; 147 testimonials inscribed on vellum ; 73 testimonials inscribed on parchment ; 39 pecuniary rewards, with certificates.

Cases in 1888.

NUMBER OF AWARDS FOR RESCUES OR ATTEMPTED RESCUES— NUMBER OF PERSONS RESCUED.

It is a very remarkable fact that the list of persons to whom awards have been made embrace almost every rank of life, including officers and men in the army, navy, volunteers, police, clergymen, professional men, tradesmen, laborers, school boys and girls, ladies, and even female domestic servants, showing that human virtue is no respecter of persons.

Should any of my readers wish to help in the noble work of this most deserving Society, they can communicate with the Secretary, Captain I. W. Home, 4 Trafalgar Square, Charing Cross, London, England.

To the Royal Humane Society.

All honor to the men of brain,
 Who first conceived the plan
Of restoring to life again
 An almost drowned man.

Through your instructions we can gain
 That victory over death,
Which makes the heart revive again
 And gives the nostrils breath.

Your noble acts the world records
 Upon its scroll of fame ;
Where actions speak more loud than words,
 We find your honored name.

The medals that you oft confer
 For saving human life,
Are worn by men who them prefer
 To those of battle's strife.

Medals and Clasps of the Royal Humane Society.

> Long may your grand Society
> Reward the truly brave,
> Who risk their lives by land and sea
> Another's life to save.   —*W. D. A.*

Description of the Medals and Clasps of the Royal Humane Society.

> "The medal, faithful to its charge of fame,
> Through climes and ages bears each form and name;
> In one short view, subjected to our eye,
> Gods, emperors, heroes, sages, beauties, lie."—*Pope.*

Flame having been used, both by the ancients and moderns, as the emblem of life, and its extinction as the symbol of death, the front of the medal represents a boy blowing an extinguished torch, in the hope, as expressed by the motto, "LATEAT SCINTILLULA FORSAN," "*Peradventure a little spark may yet lie hid.*" This design appears applicable both to the person apparently dead, and to the one who endeavors to resuscitate him. Under the device is the following inscription abbreviated: "SOCIETAS LONDINI IN RESUSCITATIONEM INTERMORTUORUM INSTITUTA, MDCCLXXIV." "The (Royal Humane) Society established in London for the recovery of persons in a state of suspended animation, 1774."

The reverse of the medal exhibits a civic wreath, which was the Roman reward for saving life; the inscription round it expresses the merit which obtains this honor from the Society: "HOC PRETIUM CIVE SERVATO TULIT."—"He has obtained this reward for having saved the life of a citizen." Within the wreath is the following inscription abbreviated: "VITAM OB SERVATAM DONO DEDIT SOCIETAS REGIA HUMANA."—"The Royal Humane Society presented this gift for saving life."

There is a second reverse to the Society's medal, with the civic wreath only, which is used when the medal is presented to persons who have endeavored to save the life of others at the risk of their own, but without success; the inscription reads: "VITA PERICULO EXPOSITO DONO DEDIT SOCIETAS REGIA HUMANA."—"The Royal Humane Society presented this to ——, his life having been exposed to danger."

The clasp for the silver and bronze medals is the same in shape. It is usually awarded to those who are in possession of the medal, for a second act of bravery in saving life. The author has received the Society's medal and two additional clasps.

CHAPTER XLV.

THE MASSACHUSETTS HUMANE SOCIETY.

Established 1785.

This society was established as far back as the year 1785, a few years later than the Royal Humane Society, and with similar objects — to reward deeds of bravery in saving life, and to furnish information and apparatus for the recovery of persons apparently drowned. The society received its charter in the year 1791.

The United States Life-Saving Service having extended its operations all along the coast, the Humane Society has been considerably relieved thereby from maintaining many stations that had a long history of usefulness. Although this would seem to narrow the work of the Humane Society, it had an opposite tendency, by creating a friendly rivalry between the organizations. There are now on the Massachusetts coast seventy life-saving stations altogether, of which eighteen belong to the United States Service, and fifty-two to the Humane Society. It will thus be seen that this society has undertaken a large field of work, and its success has been rewarded to some extent by the State Government, which granted at different dates considerable sums to help the society to pursue its most laudable work. Private benefactors, too, have from time to time given financial support to its operations. The society, as in the case of the Royal Humane Society, provides means for life-saving

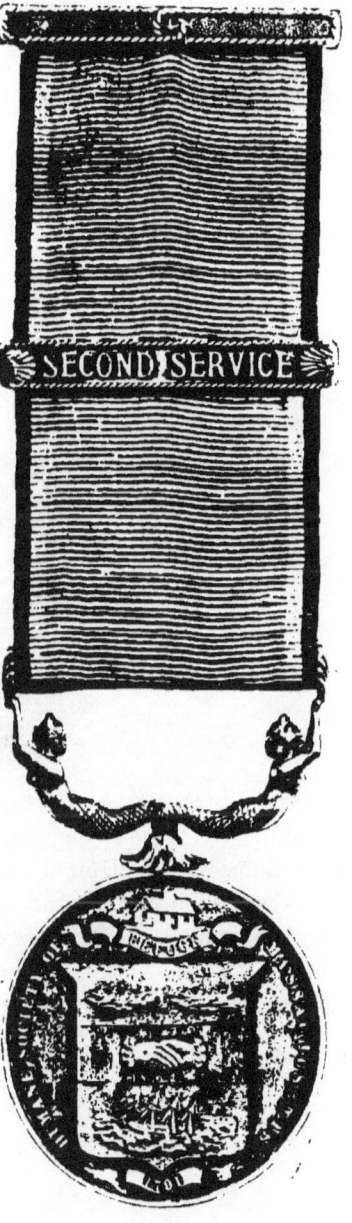

on rivers and wharfs, where traffic and bathing are sure to produce accidents. Gold, silver and bronze medals are awarded, with certificates, for conspicuous bravery in life-saving, and in needy cases money may be given to the extent of forty dollars, but not more, to one individual. The long career of noble work performed by the Massachusetts Society may be said to have been the principal factor

Medals of the Massachusetts Humane Society.

in establishing the United States Life-Saving Service, which excels all others in its complete equipment and number of its stations. Both services unite in friendly co-operation, as indeed they ought to do, having the same objects in view. The author of this work earnestly wishes God-speed to both of these noble services.

CHAPTER XLVI.

ROYAL NATIONAL LIFE-BOAT INSTITUTION.

Established 1824.

"When the loud minute-gun alarms the night,
   And plunging waters hide the bark from sight,
When lurid lightnings threat, and thunders roll,
   And roaring tempests daunt the trembling soul,—
'Tis thine, oh life-boat man, such fears to brave,
   And snatch the helpless from a watery grave."

Courage is a quality greatly to be desired, without which little good can be accomplished, but when allied to humanity it becomes truly sublime. This is particularly true with regard to life-boat men, as the operations of the service call into existence the noblest traits of which humanity is capable. The history of the Royal National Life-Boat Institution, of Great Britain, founded in 1824, teems with deeds of heroism equal to any performed on the battle-field or elsewhere. This is the finest volunteer life-boat organization in the world. With a fleet of over four hundred life-boats, manned by their sturdy crews of fishermen, they have, amid scenes of the greatest peril, rescued over eight. thousand persons who would have perished but for their timely assistance. Since its organization, this society has awarded over one hundred gold medals, and more than one thousand silver medals, with numerous additional clasps.

CHAPTER XLVII.

THE LIFE-SAVING BENEVOLENT ASSOCIATION OF NEW YORK.

Established 1849.

In every great maritime city the sea and its dangers are objects of the deepest interest. The sea presents itself not only as a great highway for commerce, a field of boundless pleasure and profitable employment, but alas! it has ever been, and must continue to be, associated with scenes of suffering, sorrow and death. It is only in harmony, therefore, with civilization that humanity should step in, and by organization endeavor to minimize the number of accidents, and remove where possible the cause of peril; and when the worst takes place and lives are endangered, then by every means human skill can devise, regardless of cost, go forth to the rescue at all hazards. In order the better to do this, a number of merchants connected with the shipping trade of New York formed an association, which received its charter from the State in 1849. Its first endeavors were to co-operate in providing surf-boats, rockets, carronades and other apparatus for the preservation of life and property from shipwreck. It is with the greatest pleasure I can record the fact that along the shores there have ever been found available volunteer crews, who take care of the boats and stations, and turn out to work in case of need. The society and the underwriters both naturally join in encouraging these noble men by every legitimate means, so as to secure a continuation of their most honorable and voluntary service. In 1883, twenty-seven life-boat stations were maintained by this association. The Government have assisted the society with funds to the extent of over $18,000, and it has an ample list of subscribers, in which I find the insurance companies take the lead. A very valuable medium of life-saving is the life-car, invented by Captain Douglass Ottinger, of the U. S. Revenue Cutter Service, in 1849. By the use of this car many hundred lives have been saved. To the Hon. W. A. Newell, M.C., from New Jersey, belongs the honor of first moving for funds to be supplied by the treasury for the humane purpose of saving life, and since then the American Government has warmly supported the cause.

The accompanying engraving shows the obverse and reverse sides of the medal awarded by the association, with the motto, "VITA FELICIBUS AUSIS SERVATA," or "Life preserved by fortunate deeds of boldness."

CHAPTER XLVIII.

THE ALBERT MEDAL.

Established 1867.

By Royal Warrant of 12th April, 1867, two decorations were instituted, viz.: the Albert Medal of the first class, and the Albert Medal of the second class, "which" (in the language of the warrant) "we are desirous should be highly prized and eagerly sought after." That of the first class is a gold oval-shaped decoration, enamelled in dark blue, with a monogram V. and A., interlaced with an anchor erect in gold, surrounded with a garter in bronze, inscribed in raised letters of gold: "For gallantry in saving life at sea," and surmounted by a representation of the crown of His Royal Highness, the lamented Prince Consort, and suspended from a dark blue ribbon of an inch and three-eighths in width, with four white longitudinal stripes.

The medal of the second class is similar in all respects in design, but entirely of bronze, the ribbon of which is five-eighths of an inch in width, with two white longitudinal stripes.

Bars corresponding with the medals are awarded to those already in possession of the medal, for subsequent deeds of heroism, which would have earned for them the medal itself, had they not already received it. The following cases awarded the Albert Medal are selected from a list of heroes which it would be difficult to praise too much. The *Marmion*, of North Shields, drove from her anchors and stranded near Falmouth, England. There was a strong wind blowing, with squalls. The ship, being driven among the breakers, was often entirely covered with the surf, and no communication with the shore seemed possible. The master and one man died from exposure and exhaustion. James Hudson, a youth of seventeen years, volun-

teering to swim off to the vessel (although it seemed certain death to do so), the coastguard attached lines to him, and he reached the vessel and got a running gear fixed, by which six of the crew were saved. Hudson, from want of clothing, was obliged to return after being a quarter of an hour on board, and his distress was very great, as he had to pull himself hand over hand through the surf. There was still one man alive on the ship, but he was too weak to fasten on the cork jacket brought him. In this emergency, Theophilus Jones, who had a line, but no jacket or belt on, threw himself into the sea, and after several failures, succeeded in boarding the vessel, fastened the cork jacket on the survivor, and threw him into the sea, and he was safely washed ashore, as well as Jones, who suffered considerably from the cold.

SWIMMING AND LIFE-SAVING.

The records of the Albert Medal, like those of the Victoria Cross, are full of such incidents of consummate pluck—for there is hardly another word which can aptly characterize such actions as those already mentioned, and many more—such as Lieutenant Carpenter, of H. M. S. *Challenger*, who plunged into the kelp-covered sea, at the Falkland Islands, on a dark and stormy night, in search of a seaman who had fallen overboard, and after much diving brought him up safely; of Lieutenant de Sansmarez, of the *Myrmidon*, who in the shark-haunted Banana Creek of the Congo, saved another seaman's life; of Lieutenant Sandilands, who one night sprang from a height of twenty-five feet into the sea after a ship's corporal, who had fallen overboard; of Lieutenant Forbes, of the *Rapid*, who jumped overboard between Tarragona and Gibraltar, and with the lad he had risked his life to save was picked up by the boat when already sinking under the water; or of Admiral Willoughby, who rescued the man who had dropped into the water in a fit and sunk between the transport and the pier in Alexandria Harbor.

Many other instances of gallant deeds and noble self-devotion in perils, other than those of battle, might be added; but these few will serve to illustrate the deeds which win the latest of Britain's orders of merit, the Albert Medal.

CHAPTER XLIX.

UNITED STATES LIFE-SAVING SERVICE.

Established 1871.

The United States Life-Saving Service, founded by the Hon. S. I. Kimball, in 1871, is the greatest regular service in the world. The men are enlisted as in the navy, thoroughly trained, and completely equipped with the most improved life-saving apparatus known, regardless of expense, so that the best results may be expected, and, indeed, the records of the system amply testify they are more than realized.

There are over two hundred stations along the Atlantic and Pacific seaboard, and the shores of the great lakes, manned by brave men, who patrol the beach by day and night, always on the look out for opportunity to help if help be needed. Since its organization, 38,853 lives have been saved by it, and property to the value of $55,297,652. This is a grand testimonial to its usefulness.

The distinctions awarded for life-saving by this Service are over one hundred gold medals and over two hundred silver medals, besides clasps and money awards.

Many of the rescues effected by the American crews have enveloped them in a blaze of heroism.

CHAPTER L.

OUR LIFE-SAVING SERVICE.

The Life-Saving Service of Canada is still in its infancy, though with very limited resources its members have done noble work on many trying occasions.

It is to be hoped that such a commendable expenditure of public money will very soon be heartily endorsed by our legislature, and that the executive will be empowered to organize a really efficient service on something like a scale worthy of the cause, and creditable to the country.

Toronto Harbor Life-Saving Crew.

From TORONTO EVENING NEWS, *of October 12th,* 1885.

"In May, 1883, Captain Andrews, in company with Island Constable Ward (who has also distinguished himself in saving many lives from drowning), organized the Toronto Harbor Life-Saving Crew, to man the life-boat recently transferred from the harbor trust to the Dominion Government, under the direction of the Minister of Marine. The crew go out for practice fourteen times every season, in all kinds of weather, and consequently have acquired considerable proficiency in the launching and management of the life-boat, and are rowing a powerful, even stroke, with a perfect regularity of movement. Since the establishment of this life-saving crew, they have been instrumental in rescuing a large number of persons from drowning, which services have been suitably recognized by the presentation of medals and clasps from the Royal Humane Society, and valuable binocular glasses from the Canadian Government, besides other life-saving testimonials. It is hoped that Capt. Andrews' recommendation to convert this first-class volunteer crew into a regular life-saving crew will be acted upon at once by those in authority, and a complete life-saving station established in this city, with a salaried crew, drilled and equipped in the same manner as they are in the United States Life-Saving Service."

The Life Boat.

Dedicated to the Minister of Marine and my comrades in the service.

Man the life-boat! loudly they cry,
 I know that call right well;
Thou ark of mercy, how shall I
 Thy deeds of glory tell?

When with my comrades brave and true,
 We launch upon the wave,
To rescue some poor shipwreck'd crew,
 Whose lives we seek to save.

What, though the hurricane may roar,
 And angry waves assail,
We'll pull still stronger with the oar
 Regardless of the gale.

And though the storm-king's forces do
 Their utmost to defeat,
We reach the wreck, take off the crew,
 And make our work complete.

God bless the life-boat and her crew,
 And may they ever be
Faithful and true their work to do,
 Like heroes of the sea.

—W. D. A.

CHAPTER LI.

LIFE-SAVING APPLIANCES.

Captains of vessels should exercise their crews frequently in lowering and hoisting the life-boats during fair and rough weather, assigning each man a certain place with certain duties. By this means each man will become familiar with his special duty, and when the time of peril comes, will be enabled to perform it without excitement, thus, in a great measure, preventing what is known as a panic launch.

The coolness of officers and men in such cases adds materially to the preservation of life

There are numerous life-saving appliances, such as cork life preservers, ring buoys, etc., etc. These should always be kept in convenient places, easy of access to passengers and crew.

The proper method of fastening on a life preserver is to see that the shoulder straps are crossed over the shoulders tightly, while the strings are securely tied.

In the case of ladies and young or old people, life preservers should be secured to the person by some one thoroughly reliable, if possible. Put the life preservers on like a vest, cross the shoulder straps like a pair of braces, and then fasten the strings in front firmly.

Harbor Boards, and owners of wharfs should also amply provide against accidents by always having, as handy as possible, such appliances as prudence will dictate may be required, more especially in places where crowds of persons are likely to be expected; under such circumstances the greatest care should be exercised, and it is highly expedient that only experienced men should be employed around excursion boats and docks. An awkward man, not up to his work, may innocently do great harm.

It would be very useful to festoon a chain around all docks, so that a person falling into the water might have something to cling to until assistance arrived.

September 15th, 1881.—The writer exhibited a peculiar life-saving invention which Alderman Boswell, of Toronto, brought with him from England. It consisted of a chemical preparation enclosed in a tinfoil case, put in linen pockets inserted in the breast of a lady's dress or a gentleman's coat, covered with rubber, except at the bottom, to prevent water descending or touching it, when caught in rain or otherwise exposed to wet weather; but when by accident or design a person be precipitated into the water, the ascending water from beneath, coming in contact with the chemical, causes it to inflate, producing a bladder-like formation before and behind, capable of supporting the body in a very easy posture for fifty-five hours.

This test was made in Lake Ontario, opposite the Exhibition grounds, in the presence of officers of that institution and thousands of spectators, and proved entirely satisfactory. This was the first occasion on which the invention was tested in Canada, and the Rev. Cowell Brown, M.A., of Sheffield, England, the inventor, has, by his ingenuity, well earned the distinction of the bronze medal from the Exhibition Committee of Toronto.

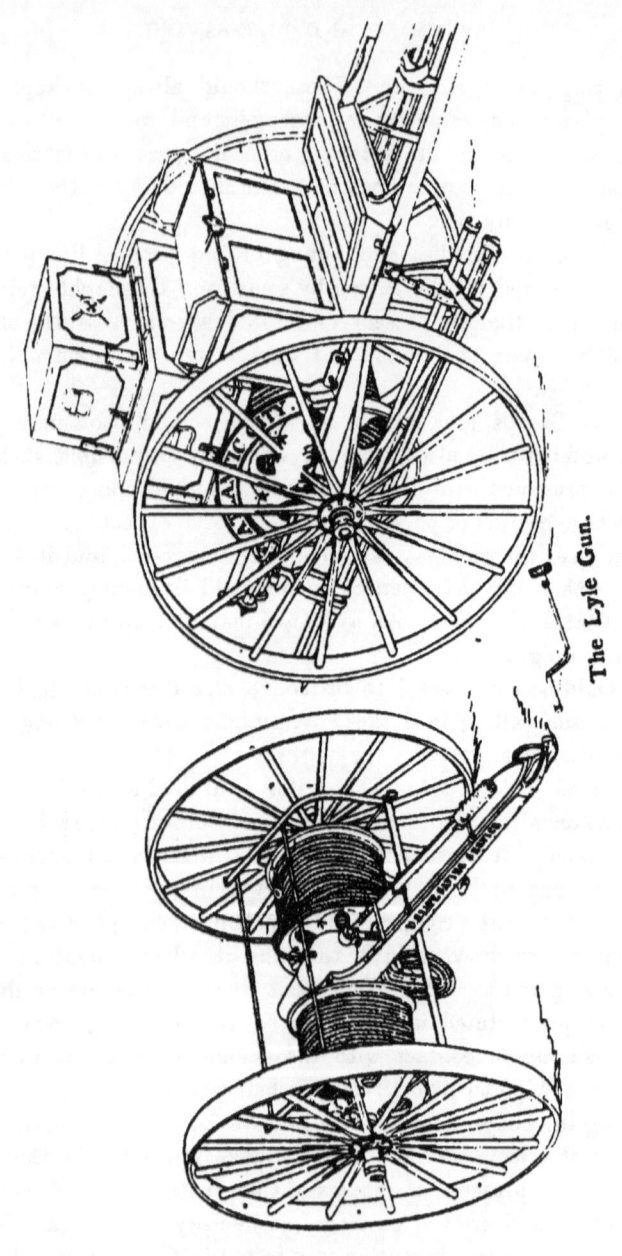

The Lyle Gun.

CHAPTER LII.

THE LYLE GUN.

The gun is the invention of Captain D. A. Lyle, of the United States Army Ordnance Department, and was approved and adopted by the United States Life-Saving Service, after a most careful series of experiments had conclusively proved its superiority over those in use, and its suitability to the requirements of the Service. It is made entirely of bronze, $2\frac{1}{2}$ in. smooth-bore, with a range of 695 yards, or nearly half a mile, and is capable of being fired with great accuracy. It weighs about 185 pounds. In action, the gun is placed in line with the wreck, and on being fired, the shot, with its line attached, goes flying over the wreck into the sea beyond; the line falls across a friendly spar or rope, and is soon seized by the sailors aboard the stranded vessel, and soon communication with the shore is established, and the "breeches-buoy" (which is simply a round ring life-preserver with a pair of trunks attached), or life-car, is got in motion, and by their means the persons endangered are hauled ashore.

McLellan's Apparatus Waggon.

This is the invention of Lieutenant McLellan, of the United States R.M. Lieutenant McLellan, as a District Superintendent of the United States Life-Saving Service, had learned by experience what was really wanted to secure complete efficiency in transport, and has succeeded in producing a waggon presenting all possible advantages. It is made in two parts, each part with two wheels, and either can be used separately, or, when necessary, both together, which carries everything required to carry out rescue work, including the Lyle gun. The construction generally is so well contrived that great speed can be accomplished in getting to work, and there is no doubt that the waggon is a most valuable addition to the life-saving apparatus.

The Dobbins Life-Boat.

CHAPTER LIII.

THE DOBBINS LIFE=BOAT

Captain D. P. Dobbins, Superintendent in the United States Life-Saving Service at Buffalo, a few years ago designed and had built, under his own supervision, a life-boat which is self-righting, self-bailing, self-ballasting and insubmergible, besides possessing great strength, and of very moderate weight, which contributes greatly to its utility, being easy to launch, and to pull through a surf, as well as being swung with great ease at a ship's davits; or, if need be, pitched from the deck of a vessel into the water, where it immediately rights itself, and can carry twenty-five to thirty-five persons out of danger, or if properly controlled, one hundred human beings can be kept afloat by it. The inventor's ingenuity, linked, as it undoubtedly is, to a broad and generous spirit of humanity, has been amply rewarded by the complete establishment of all the advantages he stated his boat possessed.

Under every possible circumstance that could happen, his boat has triumphantly maintained its superior excellence in every point, so that it is not surprising the United States Government has patronized this worthy and patriotic officer's valuable invention by ordering many of his boats for its Life-Saving Service; and our Canadian Government also, having indisputable evidence of their great superiority, has purchased life-boats from Captain Dobbins; and these have, after repeated severe tests, proved thoroughly reliable.

Captain Dobbins had learned from long experience what a life-boat really should be to deserve the name, and for many years studied carefully how to produce a boat possessing the necessary qualities. Though it took much time, much labor, and considerable expenditure of money, making experiments, the object so earnestly and patiently sought for was at length accomplished; and, as Captain Dobbins has secured letters patent for the United States, Canada, and Great

Britain, it is safe to predict that, as the virtues of the boat becomes known, the invention will prove a valuable one. The captain's general genial qualities are so widely known, that it may be safely said he is one of the most popular men in America.

The illustration on page 118 shows the life-boat on its transport waggon, which is also Captain Dobbins' own invention.

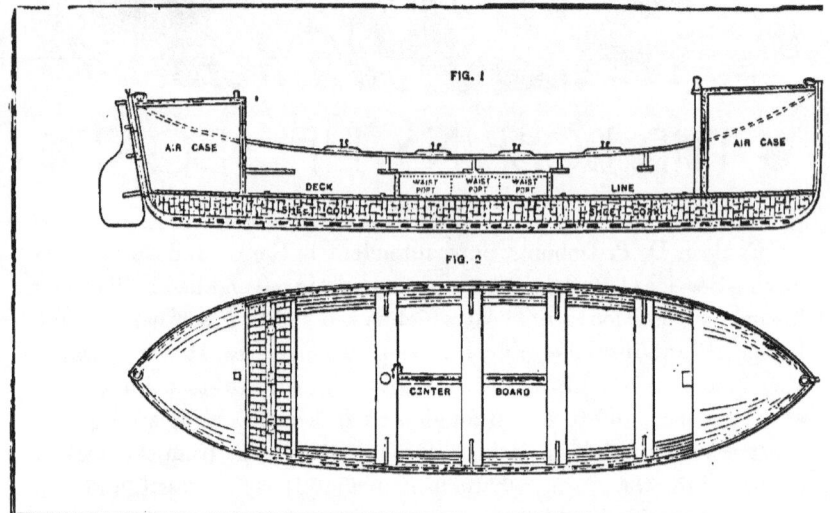

Section and Plan of the Dobbins Life-Boat.

Descriptive Particulars.

Length, 26 ft.; gross weight, about 2,000 lbs.; carvel-built, of best clear Norway pine. The buoyant ballast, made of sheet-cork, water-proofed, fills the hold beneath the water-line, solid to the exclusion of air or water-space, renders the boat absolutely proof against staving, leakage or crushing—in fact, a cork boat inside a wooden shell. It is constructed with air chambers at each end. They are entered through the man-holes and water-tight doors, and in them females, invalids and children may be put to protect them from exposure; benches for the stronger sex are also placed between the thwarts on each side. The air-chambers with the ballast right the boat immediately, if capsized, while the water flows off the deck through the automatic waist-ports in a few seconds.

Another illustration (page 122) shows the Dobbins life-boat under sail. It is provided with "partners" and "steps" for two masts, on

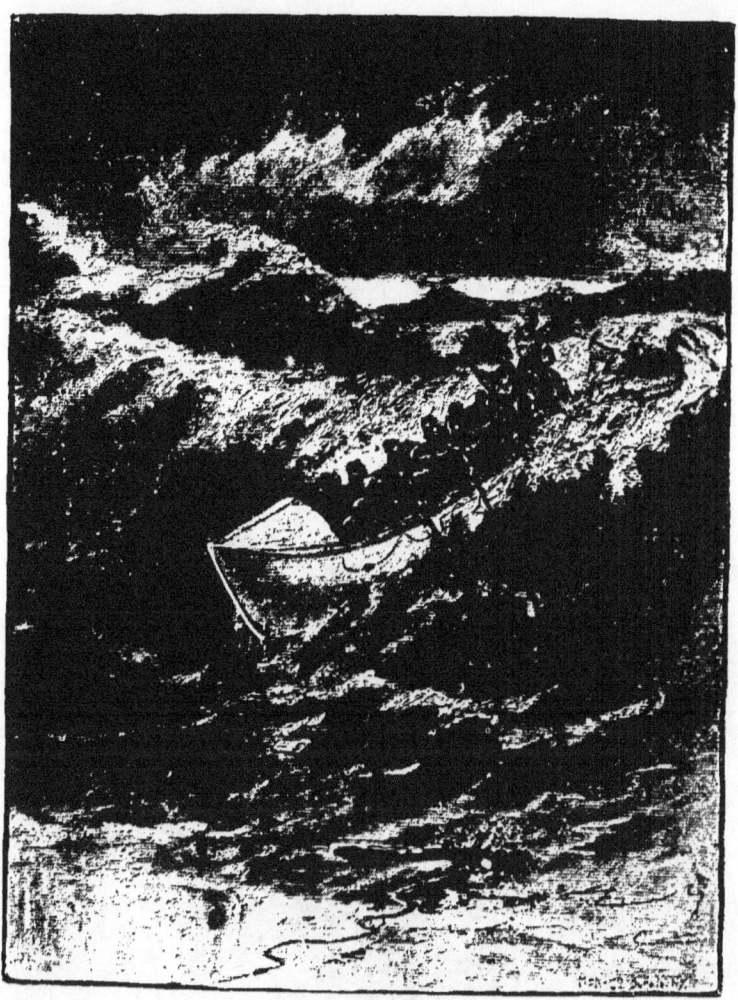

Landing in the Surf.

which to set suitable fore and aft lug sails for use in long distance or outlying shoal cruising.

The boat is built, under Captain Dobbins' personal supervision, by Messrs. Wm. Hinckson & Son, of Buffalo, N.Y.

A Remarkable Test.

From the BUFFALO COURIER, *October* 27, 1887.

"In saving the crew of the *Zack Chandler* the life-saving crew of Cleveland demonstrated in a most emphatic way that the Dobbins life-boat is all that is claimed for it. The *Chandler* went ashore during the terrible storm of last Monday morning, about fifteen miles east

The Dobbins Life-Boat under Sail.

of the Cleveland station. Captain Goodwin, the life-station keeper, being notified by telephone, engaged a locomotive and two flat cars to take his boat, waggon and beach apparatus to Noble, a station about one and a half miles from the wreck. A shot line was fired over the vessel, but her crew were too exhausted to haul out the whip-line. Then the life-boat was dragged on her bottom down a bluff bank of clay and boulders to the water. In thus dragging her and launching her over the sharp rocks her bottom was badly used up — practically destroyed. Capt. Goodwin and his men knew their boat

Going to the Rescue.

—that she would float without any bottom planking at all. They rowed to the vessel, the wind blowing about forty miles an hour and tremendous seas running, and brought the exhausted sailors safely to shore in a Dobbins boat with a stove bottom.

"Such a test of a life-boat was probably never before made. It shows conclusively that the Dobbins boat is insubmergible, no matter how badly she may be stove. The result would have been the same if there had also been holes knocked in her sides. These boats have a shallow hold, which is stowed solidly with water-proofed Spanish cork and covered with a strong deck. This makes them absolutely unsinkable. Their self-righting, self-bailing and other excellent qualities need not be mentioned here. Our fellow-townsman has good reason to feel proud over this achievement of his untiring labors in behalf of humanity."

Before closing this chapter, I wish to bear my testimony to the immense value of Captain Dobbins' most successful invention. I can consistently say, after an experience of nearly twenty years in the mercantile and life-saving services, that the Dobbins life-boat surpasses all others—in fact, it is a marvel of naval architecture. To Captain Williams, of the Buffalo Life-Boat Station, and his gallant crew, I am personally indebted for many acts of kindness during my sojourn there. To John L. Hornberger I also acknowledge my indebtedness for numerous acts of friendship.

CHAPTER LIV.

ALWAYS READY.

As it is proposed by the Canadian Government to model our life-saving service after the manner that has proved so effective in the United States, some details of the *modus operandi* adopted in that country will be read with interest, and the writer being familiar with the Cleveland station, will select that interesting port as the scene to exhibit to the reader.

The well-known port of Cleveland is situated on the south shore of Lake Erie, State of Ohio. It is one of the most important of all the ports on the great lakes. The city has a population of over 280,-000. Its numerous industries, among which are iron, coal, grain, stone, etc., produce employment for every description of vessels. The city is remarkable for the enterprise of its merchants and traders generally, and possesses some splendid specimens of architecture. The stone viaduct, which spans the cleft between the two mountains, is a magnificent structure, which was seven years in course of construction, and cost over seven million dollars. There are numerous squares and avenues, the principal of which is Euclid Avenue, over eight miles in length, and of great breadth. It is said to be the finest street in the union.

The life-saving station is situated on the west pier (inner side); it is a plain, substantial building, and picturesque, provided with an annex containing the fire boat, for service at any fire that may arise along the wharfs, or among the shipping in the harbor. How useful such a boat would be in Toronto, or indeed in any of our ports. With such a provision, should a fire unfortunately break out on the Esplanade for instance, a properly equipped and manned boat could play on the fire from the Bay, while the fire brigade operated from the land.

The first floor contains the boat-room, where the apparatus is stored, and a second smaller apartment, which is the living-room of the crew. On the second story are three or four rooms; one is appropriated for the lighter apparatus, medicine chest—an important feature in this humane work—a library, official books and papers, etc., all of which are inspected regularly.

On the floor of the boat-room that slopes toward two river doors, are the great English life-boat, and the American surf-boat. Over the latter, suspended by ropes and pulleys, the celebrated Dobbins boat hangs. The life-car slung on a rope, as if for instant service, hangs beside it. The surf-boat has seen the most service, although the Dobbins life-boat, which is fully described elsewhere, has a remarkably good record at this station.

The apparatus-room opens from the boat-room. It contains the Lyle gun and carriage, with breeches-buoy, hauling and whip lines, tally boards, crotch, blocks, and general service gear for the rescue of shipwrecked persons from stranded vessels. A mast with cross-arms stands in the harbor behind the station, for the purpose of practising with the apparatus. The sitting-room is a large and comfortable apartment. The dormitory is above it, and has two ante-rooms; one is the sleeping-room for No. 1, who takes rank next the captain, the other is the office. A short flight of stairs leads from the dormitory to the "look-out" on the roof. On the look-out is a binnacle, containing a lamp, compass, marine clock, binocular glasses, barometer and thermometer, also a ship's bell on which the watches are struck, as on man-of-war vessels. Any alarm is announced to the station by the same medium. A flagstaff surmounts the building, from which storm and weather signals are displayed. Two hours is the length of each watch on the look-out. At night the beach between the station and the foot of the breakwater is constantly patrolled. On leaving the look-out, the man on watch patrols the beach until his successor has relieved him. Each patrolman carries a watchman's time detector and a case of Costin signal-lights. The time detector is a small but effective piece of mechanism

The only keys with which the registry is effected are locked in iron cases, in posts at each end of the route. The patrolman carries the key of these iron boxes. The Costin lights are a species of Roman candle. One light cautions vessels when too near the beach, and the other calls help from the station. Be the night dark or clear, or the waves gentle or fierce, a watchful man constantly picks his way along the rough shore of the harbor beach; and day or night, in fair weather or foul, a sharp eye scans every visible object on the lake, so long as there is a chance that lives and property they guard may be placed in jeopardy. At night the duties of the patrol become severe, and often dangerous. The interval between sunset and sunrise is divided into three watches, and in case of danger to vessels the patrolmen fire their signals, and warn the ships of their peril.

When a vessel is driven ashore, the patrolman, ascertaining the fact, takes the initiatory steps in

The Operation of Rescue

by first firing his Costin signal, which emits a red flame burning for several minutes, and hastens to make his report to the keeper, who decides what is to be done. If it is decided to reach the vessel by water, the crew proceed to the boat-room where the surf-boat, always in a state of readiness, is found resting on ways provided with rollers. The crew then range themselves on either side of the surf-boat so as to jump into their places the moment the word of command is given. At this signal the men spring into their seats, the wide doors of the boat-room fly open, and the graceful craft, *fully manned and equipped*, glides into her native element and is off on her "errand of mercy." If the wreck is well inshore, the mortar cart is ordered out. This is drawn by the men where horses are not provided. While at practice, before every drill, the men are obliged to repeat off by heart their particular part of the work in rescuing the shipwrecked by means of the Lyle gun and beach apparatus. So trained they are enabled, when called out for actual service, to perform their duty well and with alacrity. Reaching the scene of the wreck, each man, well trained to his particular duty, proceeds to handle and place in position that portion of the apparatus assigned to him as his especial charge. Simultaneously the different members already "told off" load the Lyle gun, place the shot box in position, dispose the hauling gear, lines and hawser for running, attach the breeches buoy, and put the tackles in place ready for hauling; and with pick and spade begin the digging of a trench for the sand anchor, while the beach lantern upon the mortar cart throws its light upon the scene. And now the gun, which has been placed in line with the wreck, is fired; the shot, with its line attached, goes flying over the wreck into the sea beyond, and is soon secured by the sailors on board. The life-savers then bend on the whip, an endless line with two blocks attached, to the outer tail-block of which a tallyboard is fastened, previously joined to the shore end of the shot line, already being hauled in by those on board. The whip passes rapidly

Toward the Wreck,

and on arriving there the sailors make fast the tail block of the whip to the mast, well up in accordance with the printed instructions on the tally-board, and show a signal to the shore.

The life savers now bend on a strong hawser to the lower line of the whip, and by hauling on the upper line the hawser is drawn rapidly out to the wreck. Attached to the bight of the hawser is a second tally-board, which directs how and where the end of the hawser should be secured to the wreck. The tackles are now attached to the sand anchor, and the shore end of the hawser is straight and taut, when it is lifted several feet in the air and further tightened by the erection of a wooden crotch, which constitutes a temporary pier, the wreck answers for another, while the hawser line forms the suspension bridge connecting them.

A snatch-block is then thrown across the hawser, to which the breeches-buoy is attached. The ends of the whip are made fast to each side of the buoy, and it is drawn by means of the whip out toward the wreck, travelling the upgrade empty, and coming down with greater velocity with the person rescued, and by this means brought safe to shore. The life-car is frequently used in place of the breeches-buoy, when there are many women or children to be saved, or invalids, or a large number of persons to be rescued with despatch.

In bringing this paragraph to a close, I take this opportunity of acknowledging the kindness of Captain C. C. Goodwin to myself personally when serving under him, and also the very friendly feeling always exhibited toward me by the Cleveland Life-Boat crew. Captain Goodwin and his gallant crew have each been awarded the United States life-saving gold medal of the first class for their repeated successful acts of heroism.

THE SQUARE AND COMPASS.

To Captain C. C. Goodwin and Crew of the United States Life-Saving Service.

The following lines were written by an old veteran in the craft, on witnessing the noble work performed by the Cleveland Life-Saving crew in the rescue of over eight hundred persons during the floods on the Ohio River. The rescue party were maintained during this trying ordeal by the Masonic Relief Association:

> With your blue-bannered emblems before you,
>   With strong, steady stroke of your oars,
> Up and onward the wild waters bore you,
>   Afloat to our desolate doors.
>
> You came to us, brothers, like brothers,
>   With silent, yet eloquent deed,
> With helpful hands held out to others
>   As friends of the needy in need.
>
> And here with the torrent around us,
>   Our bosoms despondent and dumb,
> You came in your kindness and found us,
>   As fearless faith said you would come.
>
> Go back, bonny boat, with our blessing,
>   Our hearts are as full as the flood;
> Distress itself ceases distressing,
>   In the goodness of witnessing good.
>
> If our shirts were a kite still we'd fly it,
>   To honor that brotherly crew;
> If our hats were a crown, yet we'd shy it,
>   To cheer for your banner of blue.
>
> You may raise in your wrath, cruel river,
>   But high above flood-reach we'll stand;
> The square and the compass for ever,
>   The lion's-paw grip of the hand.

Masonic Hall, Newport, Kentucky,
  February, 1883.

CHAPTER LV.

"ONE OF THE MEN WE KNOW."

A GREAT CANADIAN SWIMMER, A CANDIDATE FOR THE ALBERT MEDAL OF THE FIRST CLASS—DEVOTED TO A GRAND WORK.

Extracts from the Canadian and American Press.

It is always a pleasure to know a man who stands at the head of any line of endeavor. A man who excels in the particular direction to which he has turned his energies is sure to be a man worth knowing. Such a man is Capt. W. D. Andrews, the great Canadian swimmer, whose many deeds of heroism have made his name honored in this country and in Europe. In Buffalo and Cleveland, where he passed much time, he has made many personal friends. It would require a volume to describe all his sublime acts of heroism. Lakes Ontario and Erie have been the principal scenes of his exploits, and his fame has spread throughout the entire lake district.

His recent recommendation for that most distinguished honor, the Albert Medal of the first class, in recognition of his many daring acts of bravery in saving life from drowning, gives timely interest to the following sketch of his career:

Captain W. D. Andrews was born in the city of Kingston, Ont., Canada, May 19th, 1853. From his boyhood up he has been employed in one way or other upon the water, and happily for him and many others, he early in life acquired a thorough knowledge of the art of swimming. Andrews' exploits in saving life date from the year 1869, and from that time he has always been ready to risk his own life to save the lives of others. The danger incurred in jumping overboard is very great. Many expert swimmers shrink from it. Andrews has encountered this risk under almost every variety of circumstances. He has followed the drowning under rafts of timber, under vessels at anchor or in docks, from great heights, and often to the bottom in great depths of water; and, what is very remarkable, always successfully.

From his brilliant record are selected the following deeds of bravery, any one of which should entitle him to the highest honors this world can confer for saving life:

Kingston.

July 23rd, 1869.—The first deed of bravery to which attention is called occurred at his native city; when only sixteen years old he rescued a lad of eleven years of age, who, while playing on a raft of timber opposite the city, accidentally fell into the bay. Fortunately, Andrews, who was writing in an office upstairs, heard the cry, and taking in the situation at once on reaching the wharf, plunged in with all his clothes on and rescued the boy, who had sunk twice before assistance arrived. He would certainly have perished but for Andrews' bravery.

For this and other acts of gallantry Captain Andrews was awarded the gold life-saving medal of the *first class* with clasps.

In *September, 1869*, Andrews commenced steamboating, which occupation he followed for many years successfully.

Owen Sound.

On the morning of the *22nd of April, 1873*, while the mail steamer *Waubuno*, of which Captain Andrews was an officer, was lying at her moorings on the west side of the Sydenham River, opposite the city of Owen Sound, he rescued an old man who attempted to cross the river on some floating timber (the swing bridge being in course of repairs at the time). When about mid-stream the man fell into the water, where he was struggling for life, when Captain Andrews' attention was called to the circumstance. He instantly sprang into the river just as he stood, in full uniform, and swimming out to the drowning man, caught him as he rose again to the surface, and swam with him to the Owen Sound side of the river, where he landed him in safety. Then finding it impossible to procure a boat, and feeling his clothes stiffening about him in the frosty air, Andrews again plunged into the ice-cold water and swam back to the steamer, where he was received with cheers by the officers and crew, who fully appreciated his courage and humanity. For this Captain Andrews received the Owen Sound life-saving gold medal.

Toronto.

In *July 1874*, Andrews removed to Toronto, where he soon became celebrated as a first-class swimmer. On *10th July, 1878*, Andrews performed another deed of bravery in saving the life of an Englishman named William Waghorne, aged twenty-seven, who was bathing in the river Don, and got into peril. Captain Andrews heard the cry for help, ran to the spot, plunged in and saved the man. Mr. Waghorne recognized Captain Andrew's invaluable services by making him a suitable present. In addition, the city of Toronto awarded the Captain a gold medal with clasp bearing a suitable inscription.

August 26th, 1878.—Under circumstances very similar to the last case, Captain Andrews rescued a gentleman, J. L. Thompson, for which he received the Royal Humane Society's testimonial, on vellum, presented by Mayor Beatty.

April 27th, 1881.—Captain Andrews was elected President of the Dolphin Swimming Club.

July 29th, 1881.—While at practice near Hanlan's Point, he swam out to the assistance of two young men—about five hundred yards distance—and brought them safely to shore. For this he received the bronze medal of the Royal Humane Society and certificate of honor, presented by Mayor McMurrich.

September 5th, 1881.—Captain Andrews was awarded the gold cross of valor, which was presented in the City Hall, Nov. 4th, 1881, by Alderman Boswell, in the presence of a large assembly of citizens.

July 22nd, 1882.—Captain Andrews was appointed swimming master to the Wiman Island Baths. Three days later, in company with a young man named McBean, in response to a "distress" signal, he went to the assistance of six young ladies, whose overcrowded boat had shipped so much water they were in danger of drowning. When Andrews and his companion reached them, the water had already reached the thwarts, and was still coming in over the weather side; by constant baling and careful management the ladies were brought safely to shore, though there was a considerable sea on at the time; but, with the exception of a thorough drenching, and the necessary confinement at the Wiman Baths while that inconvenience was being remedied, the ladies were nothing the worse, although their position for a time was exceedingly dangerous.

September 25th, 1882.—Captain Andrews plunged into Toronto Bay, and swam out to the assistance of a young man who was seized with cramps, and was in danger; he was safely brought to shore. For this he received the Royal Humane Society's bronze clasp and certificate of honor, presented by Mayor McMurrich.

May, 1883.—Captain Andrews, in company with Island Constable Ward, organized the Toronto Harbor Life-Saving Crew, to man the life-boat recently transferred from the Harbor Trust to the Dominion Government, under the control of the Minister of Marine.

July 27th, 1883.—During a tremendous storm, exceeding in violence anything that has been seen on Toronto Bay for years, Captain Andrews, in company with William Ward and John D. Patry, accomplished another noble rescue. While the storm was at its height, these three brave men put out in Dr. Oldright's open skiff at the imminent risk of their lives to the rescue of Professor Schlochow, a German music teacher, whose boat was capsized, and who was clinging for his life to the keel, while every wave washed over his head. In their eager efforts to reach the drowning man the stroke-oar was broken, which threw the boat into the trough of the sea, when the next wave filled her completely, and they had to put ashore at Sandy Point to empty her. Nothing daunted, however, they made a fresh start, and after the greatest exertion they reached the capsized craft, and taking off the drowning man, placed him in the bottom of the boat and pulled for the shore, again landing at the lake-side opposite the shelter, after a pull of nearly three miles. They carried the unconscious form of the man into the Wiman Island Baths, where Drs. Geikie and Bell, who were among the hundreds of spectators, instantly set to work to resuscitate the rescued man, and after long and continued exertions, his rescuers had the gratification of seeing him restored to consciousness. This constitutes the very best case of life-saving which has ever taken place in Toronto Bay. Such was the fury of the storm—the public observatory places the velocity of the wind at eighty miles an hour—and the rolling of the sea, and so enormous were the troughs of the waves into which the little craft momentarily fell, that she could only be seen from the shore when she rose buoyantly upon the crest of the waves, and the heavy rainstorm that prevailed at the time greatly added to the peril of the situation. Indeed, the many people who witnessed the occurrence aver that the conduct of these brave men in their gallant and successful effort to save life, was worthy of every commendation. In recognition of his bravery on this occasion, the Royal Humane Society forwarded a bronze clasp and its certificate of honor to his Worship, the then Mayor, A. R. Boswell, Esq., who presented them to Captain Andrews during the City Council meeting on 18th January, 1884, amid the applause of the council.

Suitable awards were also made to Messrs. Ward and Patry by the Royal Humane Society.

SWIMMING AND LIFE-SAVING.

The Mayor, in making the presentation, congratulated Captain Andrews on being the recipient of these honors from so noble a society, as well as being one of three citizens of whose bravery Toronto was proud.

This is the fourth recognition by the Royal Humane Society of Captain Andrews' bravery in life-saving from drowning.

March 4th, 1884.—The circumstances of this rescue having been reported to the Minister of Marine, the act of the three brave men recorded received the marked approbation of the Dominion Government, who unanimously voted in the open House that a suitable testimonial be presented to each. This testimonial took the form of Binocular Glasses, with inscription on Captain Andrews' pair as follows:

"*Presented to* CAPTAIN W. D ANDREWS *by the Government of Canada in recognition of his humane exertions in saving life on Toronto Bay, 27th July, 1883.*"

The presentation took place in the council chamber at a regular meeting. The Mayor, in making the presentation, said that he hoped they might each live long to enjoy the glory of that hazardous rescue, and that when again required they might be equally successful in their attempts to save human life. Each of the men made suitable replies.

In addition to this proud distinction, the Dolphin Swimming Club also presented Captain Andrews with a magnificent gold medal suitably inscribed; the design being a round gold life preserver with lines attached, suspended by a gold clasp bearing the word "TORONTO."

This medal was presented by Captain J. L. Rawbone in the Club Rooms, 95 King St. East, on behalf of the general body of members.

During the Semi-Centennial year, 1884, Captain Andrews frequently distinguished himself in saving life from drowning, each rescue being suitably acknowledged by the Minister of Marine. The following is a copy of one of the letters:

"DOMINION OF CANADA,
"MARINE DEPARTMENT,
"*Ottawa,* 22nd Sept., 1884.

"SIR,—The Department has noted with much satisfaction a paragraph in the Toronto *Mail* of the 8th July last, in which reference is made to your action in rescuing two persons who had drifted out towards the eastern gap in an apparently helpless condition, and I am to convey to you the thanks of the Minister of Marine for the services rendered on the occasion referred to.

"I am, sir, your most obedient servant,

"WILLIAM SMITH,
"Deputy Minister of Marine.

"CAPTAIN ANDREWS,
"Life Saving Station, Toronto."

August 5th, 1884.—Captain Andrews plunged in with all his clothes on to the rescue of a young lad named Edward Lawson, who was in danger of drowning in Toronto Bay, near the eastern point of the Island. On this occasion, the gallant little fellow, burdened with the weight of his wet clothing, especially his boots, which had become filled with water, sank with the boy, who was nearly as large as himself; rising to the surface, however, he struck out again for the shore, pluckily retaining his hold of the boy whom he risked his life to save.

Reaching shallow water, he was met by Captain Ward, who waded out to meet him, in company with Mr. J. B. Marshall. The boy was taken to Mrs. Marshall's restaurant, where he received every attention, and speedily recovered. Before leaving, the boy thanked the Captain for saving his life, and subsequently Andrews received suitable acknowledgments from Edward Lawson the rescued lad, David Mills his companion, and the Hon. Wm. Smith, Deputy Minister of Marine.

August 18th, 1884.—Captain Andrews jumped in with all his clothes on, and rescued a little girl near the same place.

August 25th, 1884.—Rescued a lady from drowning in the Bay near the ferry wharf.

July 1st, 1885.—In company with Captain Ward, went to the assistance of four persons capsized from a small boat on Lake Ontario, about a mile and a half from the eastern point of the Island. After a long, hard pull, they reached the scene of the accident, where they found a number of boats collected, one of which contained the two survivors, a lady and gentleman. They were taken in tow. Immediately on reaching the shore they were transferred to Ward's Hotel, where Captain Andrews put in operation the rules for reviving the apparently drowned, and in less than half an hour succeeded in restoring them to consciousness. After receiving every care and attention from Mrs. Ward, they left for home the same evening. Subsequently Captain Andrews received a Christmas present from the young man bearing the following inscription :

"To Captain W. D. Andrews,

"In grateful remembrance,

"FRANK J. OTTER."

July 21st, 1885.—Rescued a young man from drowning in the Bay near the eastern gap.

August 11th, 1885.—Jumped in with his clothes on, and rescued a boy from drowning near the Wiman Baths, receiving the thanks of his parents, both of whom were present.

In addition to these there are many others, replete with the same good qualities, and doing equal honor to this sturdy saver of life.

Buffalo.

From the BUFFALO EXPRESS, 10*th December*, 1886.

"In the fall of 1885, Captain Andrews resolved to devote himself to a worthy mission. He came to Buffalo in order to acquire a practical knowledge of the methods adopted and in use by the United States Life-Saving Service in rescuing the shipwrecked.

"In this city Captain Andrews was received by Captain D. P. Dobbins, the courteous Superintendent of the Ninth District, in whose company he visited Kingston's boat-building establishment, where he witnessed one of Captain Dobbins' celebrated life-boats in process of construction. He visited the Buffalo Life-Saving Station, where he immediately entered upon his mission, attending all the drills and exercises daily, soon acquiring a sound theoretical knowledge of every detail of the service. Believing, however, that the only way to obtain a thorough practical knowledge of every branch of the service would be by entering the Life-Saving Service as a regular surf-man, he resolved to do so, asking as a special favor to be sent to the most dangerous port on the lakes, where he would be most likely to see plenty of genuine life-boat work. Being a British subject, it was necessary for him to obtain special permission from the Government at Washington to join any American life-saving crew. This was readily granted, and his application was turned over to Superintendent Dobbins, who assigned him to duty at

Cleveland.

Here Captain Andrews' services were almost immediately called into requisition.

"Shortly after midnight, on the very night of his arrival, in company with the other members of the life-saving crew, he was summoned to the rescue of the schooner *J. R. Pelton*, of Cleveland, bound from Toledo, O., for her home port in ballast, with a crew of five men, which dragged her anchors during a heavy north-east gale, and was rapidly drifting on to the beach. Both vessel and crew were brought into harbor in safety. Subsequently Captain Andrews, in company with the Cleveland life-boatmen, rendered valuable assistance to the propeller *E. S. Shieldon*, and others.

"*December 15th, 1885.*—Captain Andrews received a 'first-class certificate of competency' from Keeper Goodwin, of the Cleveland station, and on the *18th* a certificate of proficiency from Supt. Dobbins, who declared him 'qualified for any position in the life-saving service.'

"Captain Andrews has made this his life-work, and has perfected himself in every essential requirement necessary to the very best results. Although not of very large stature, he is a strong and fearless swimmer, with a quick eye and a cool head, which enable him to go at his work in a confident and ready manner. The Canadian Government are considering the advisability of converting their present volunteer life-saving service into a regular paid service, like that of the United States. Captain Andrews is prominently mentioned for instructor and superintendent of the service when established, a post which he is eminently qualified to fill.

"Since his return to Toronto, he has again been instrumental in saving life."

www.ingramcontent.com/pod-product-compliance
Lightning Source LLC
Chambersburg PA
CBHW022134160426
43197CB00009B/1281